STAGING STEINBECK

STAGING STEINBECK

DRAMATISING
THE GRAPES OF WRATH

PETER WHITEBROOK

CASSELL
LONDON

Cassell Publishers Limited
Artillery House, Artillery Row
London   SW1P 1RT

First published 1988

British Library Cataloguing in Publication Data

Whitebrook, Peter, *1952–*
    Staging Steinbeck : dramatising *The
    Grapes of Wrath.*
    1. Fiction in English. American writers.
    Steinbeck, John, 1902–1968. Grapes of wrath.
    Dramatisation
    I. Title
    813'.52

ISBN 0 304 32199 0

Typeset by Inforum Ltd, Portsmouth
Printed and bound in Great Britain by
Mackays of Chatham plc,
Chatham, Kent

For Vivien

John Steinbeck's *The Grapes of Wrath*, adapted by Peter Whitebrook and Duncan Low, was first performed by American Festival Theatre at the Netherbow Theatre, Edinburgh, as part of the Edinburgh International Festival Fringe, on 10 August 1987. The cast was as follows:

USED-CAR SALESMAN/GAS-STATION MAN/ FLOYD KNOWLES/HIGGINS/SECOND MAN WITH CASY	David Beggs
PA JOAD	Albert S. Bennett
GRANMA JOAD	Dorothy Bernard
CONNIE RIVERS	Paul Binotto
AGGIE WAINWRIGHT/YOUNG GIRL	Heather Hitt
TRACTOR MAN/TEXAN/COP AT HOOVERVILLE/ WALLACE/FIRST MAN WITH CASY/THIRD GUARD AT HOOPER'S RANCH	Matthew Gallagher
MA JOAD	Faith Geer
OWNER MAN/NOAH JOAD/PERSKY/FIRST GUARD AT HOOPER'S RANCH	Damien Kavanagh
JIM CASY	George McGrath
YOUNG GIRL IN BARN	Miranda McGrath
ROSE OF SHARON RIVERS	Chris Ann Moore
TENANT/IVY WILSON/SHERIFF BIRD/SECOND GUARD AT HOOPER'S	Duard Mosley
SAIRY WILSON/MRS THOMAS	Sandy Spatz
TOM JOAD	Peter Spears
AL JOAD	Temple Williams

Directed by Rob Mulholland

Costumes designed by Sue Ellen Rohrer

Set designed by Janet Scarfe

Produced by Harold Easton

ACKNOWLEDGEMENTS

I am grateful to McIntosh and Otis, Inc., New York, for permission to quote from the stage version of *The Grapes of Wrath* by Peter Whitebrook and Duncan Low, and from the novel by John Steinbeck.

The production photographs of the play are reproduced by courtesy of American Festival Theatre.

I also wish to thank Barry Holmes at Cassell, London. His advice, encouragement, enthusiasm, and wit has been the most invaluable guide and support during the preparation of this book.

INTRODUCTION

During the year I spent adapting John Steinbeck's 1939 novel, *The Grapes of Wrath*, into a stage play, working in script meetings with Duncan Low (who had suggested the project), and with the director and the dramaturg, and later in rehearsals with the director and actors in preparation for its three-week run at the Edinburgh Festival Fringe, I found myself on an exciting, utterly engulfing, complex, and often unpredictable journey. Bursts of arts journalism staved off enquiring letters from my bank as *The Grapes* took over my life.

Part of the road to the play was the search for Steinbeck himself. The bare facts of his life are that he was born the son of a mill-manager and a schoolteacher in Salinas, California, in 1902. The town, south of San Francisco and a few miles from Monterey on the Pacific coast, is surrounded by the region of fertile grandeur Steinbeck used as the backdrop to much of his fiction. He held a succession of labouring jobs before finding success as a writer. *The Grapes of Wrath*, which won a Pulitzer Prize in 1940, and *East of Eden* (1952), have become major landmarks in American literature; *Tortilla Flat* (1935), *Of Mice and Men* (1937), minor ones. He married three times, won the Nobel Prize for Literature in 1962 and died in 1968.

To discover Steinbeck, I re-read the important novels, and as many accounts of the man as I could find, often taking a chance and flicking through the indexes of biographies of other writers. Thus I came across, in *The Kindness of Strangers*, Donald Spoto's biography of Tennessee Williams, the morsel that Steinbeck was an admirer of Williams' work.

Research and such chance encounters as that above pieced together a platform on which I constructed not only my own interpretation of *The Grapes of Wrath*, but also my own John Steinbeck: a Steinbeck invisible but palpable, whom I sometimes imagined sitting somewhere behind me while I worked at my desk, or watching from a corner at the back of our draughty rehearsal room. I imagined a big, broad-chested man with hard-skinned hands. A man of powerful emotions, of powerful sensitivity, sentiment and rage, an observer, a man always of great curiosity.

It is now, by the way, January 1988. The play is written and performed, the journal of its making that follows this Introduction,

9

complete. I am deliberating my next project but still remain alert for Steinbeck references. And the other day, while reading *Timebends*, Arthur Miller's recently published memoirs, I found Miller's acknowledgement that in *The Grapes of Wrath*, Steinbeck had written 'scenes that were engraved on America like the Indian's profile on the nickel'. It is a particularly vibrant simile – the magnitude of Steinbeck's achievement is its absorption into the very currency of America.

Briefly, the novel, set during the Depression following the Crash of 1929 when the effervescence of the previous decade evaporated almost overnight, tells the story of migrant workers streaming out from the mid-west, refugees from the dust-storms literally blowing in great opaque clouds the topsoil and nutrition from the land they had worked as sharecroppers for generations. Their livelihood vanished into a suffocating fog of greys and browns, one that clogged truck engines to a standstill, that destroyed as quickly as the banks pulling out their investment. In 1935, two million homeless travelled the roads searching for work. The novel embraces a people on the move from arid ruin to the fertility and promises of California but homes in on one family, the Joads, from Sallisaw, Oklahoma, and Jim Casy, the ex-preacher who travels west with them on their broken-down Hudson truck.

It is a surging narrative. But it was the language that fired me. The best of Steinbeck, along with the best of Williams and Miller, is replete with a love of the rhythms and music of words. It is something, I suppose, that has always been within the structure of only the very best writing, but it is all the more important in an age in which the will to explore the full expressiveness of language is generally absent and shrunk into a few small crevices. The great writers of the past and today have always held aloft the militant torch of language. I attempted to work in its light.

The director, Rob Mulholland, once described those dust-storms as 'the greatest natural disaster ever to hit our country'. *The Grapes of Wrath* is the story of that disaster, and a further part of my quest during the writing was to discover its real, internal nature and how it was to work through the characters and the language of the play. And to me, the core of the novel is the recounting of a moral disaster. The mythology of America, of equality, of the honourable man beating a living from the environment and finding prosperity under the western sun, collapsed beyond rectification, almost beyond comprehension. Only moral outrage was left after the wind, the banks, and the giant corporations took everything else. The real disaster for the Joads – to me – was an eradication of faith, in America and in themselves as Americans, as people; and the play became – for me – a play about faith. That is why the Joads and Casy are such extraordinary creations. They are at once universal and heroic while remaining inextricably the symbols of their time and place. In their strength and vulnerability, they take their place not only among the great of literature but also as part of the architecture of the American nation.

When I started work I began keeping a journal initially to note ideas and possible directions of development, so that when questions were raised in script meetings I might, if necessary, have some sort of *aide-mémoire* to come to my rescue. As the team working on *The Grapes* grew larger, so the nature of my journey changed and the nature of the journal with it. It became a place in which, after script meetings and long rehearsals, I could wind down and record my impressions of the day's events. I wrote usually late at night, free flow on pages of A4 pad, which I then stapled together and pushed into a large envelope. I did not read back what I had written until September 1987, after the play had ended its run, after the Edinburgh Festival was over.

I have not re-written much of my original. As I thought footnotes would be distracting, I have made brief additions to early passages to identify people and places more coherently for the reader. I have tidied up grammar here and there, but nothing I have done detracts from the immediacy of what I wrote then. Neither have I, with the clarity and relative peace of hindsight, made any attempt to alter the quality of my responses to what was happening.

It remains for me to say, therefore, that the journal that follows, though I believe it an accurate reflection of the year, is my personal record of the journey I undertook with *The Grapes of Wrath*. Others who joined the project will have their own views, for no two travellers' perceptions are identical, even when it is assumed they are looking in the same direction. All I can say is that here, in this journal in my eyes at that time, is what happened.

Peter Whitebrook
Edinburgh, 1988

1986

SEPTEMBER

Thursday 25   A telephone call from Duncan Low.
He has the idea of a stage version of John Steinbeck's 1939 novel, *The Grapes of Wrath*, and putting it on at next year's Edinburgh Festival Fringe. An adaptation authorised by the Steinbeck Estate has never been done before. What do I think? I last read the book several years ago as a student and, apart from its narrative, my recollection of it is hazy. I tell him I think the adaptation itself will be a huge undertaking, quite apart from the copyright and legal problems involved.

'I've got that side sorted out.'

'Really? How?'

'Come round to the flat and talk about it. Tonight.'

I'm intrigued. Duncan and I know each other little: he has been administrator of the Netherbow Theatre in Edinburgh for some time and is now planning to set up his own freelance administration consultancy; I, meanwhile, work in arts journalism.

His mews flat is only a couple of minutes walk from my own home and, sitting on a long black couch in his lounge, the brick cobbled street darkening outside, he outlines what he has achieved so far. He has spoken to Adline Finlay of the English Theatre Guild in London, representatives of the Steinbeck Estate in this country, and to the lawyers representing the Steinbeck Estate in New York. By an extraordinary quirk of fortune, he called at the time the dramatic rights to the novel were being re-negotiated with the Steppenwolf Theatre Company of Chicago who plan, at some point, to write and produce their own version. Steppenwolf, formed by a group of graduates and undergraduates about fifteen years ago, is an impressive name both in America and Britain. The core of the original company have stayed together, committed to evolving their own style of workshopping and production, all the while fighting for the artistic recognition they now have. Lyle Kessler's *Orphans*, for which Albert Finney won a best actor award in London last year, was a Steppenwolf production.

However, Duncan has succeeded in getting exclusive authority for an adaptation to be produced for up to thirty performances in Edinburgh next year, providing that the script is approved by the Steinbeck Estate (and, presumably, by Steinbeck's widow, Mrs Elaine Steinbeck). A similar proviso will, apparently, govern any option Steppenwolf have.

'So, where do I fit in?'

'Writing it.'

Most of me jumps at the chance, part of me stays cautious. My memory of the novel is that it is intensely theatrical, but its vastness, its complexity, will present massive problems. Which is fine. One of the reasons to do it. But literary widows are reputed to be tough. So are New York lawyers. The combination sounds formidable. But if it could be done . . . And one big hurdle is already cleared . . .

I count the months. The Festival is in August, which means rehearsals in July, the Fringe programme published in June . . . A script will have to be production-ready, and approved, by April or May at the latest. It will be a tight schedule.

Duncan broaches the idea of the adaptation being produced and performed by an American company. A good proportion of my caution moves into the jump-at-it camp. As Duncan directed the Scottish première of Marsha Norman's 'Night, Mother at this year's Fringe with actors from Studio Theatre Productions, New York, he suggests contacting Hal Easton, Studio's executive producer, when we have some sort of draft ready for reading.

I know Studio's work. They've brought American drama to the Fringe for five years now, usually five or six productions each year. The company's reputation is high. This year they won a *Scotsman* Fringe First with the British première of Arthur Miller's adaptation of *Playing For Time*, Fania Fenelon's harrowing and courageous autobiographical account of playing in a Jewish women's orchestra in a Nazi death camp in which thousands were systematically gassed.

We agree that to play to respectable houses, to survive on the Fringe, where each year about eight hundred companies produce about a thousand plays, revues, and cabarets, any two of the three factors of play, author, and company must be a known quantity. Draw a blank on all three and you should think long and hard about even considering coming to Edinburgh, on two and you have a real fight on your hands, on one and you're still in for a struggle. But, if all goes well, we have a known title, a known original author, and a known company. The unknowns are us.

I promise to re-read the novel and call Duncan as soon as I've done so.

At home, I discuss the idea with Vivien. I've already made up my mind to go ahead, but her counsel is always pertinent and wise. She confirms I should do it. In fact, it's come at a particularly good time for me. A radio play I had hopes for has fallen through, and the few weeks after the Festival, after three weeks of intensive work reviewing for *The Scotsman* and BBC Radio 4's *Kaleidoscope*, are desultory, the usually cold, grey Edinburgh summer falling into colder, greyer autumn.

In September, every church hall, room above pub, function room below private club, every makeshift space in the bleakest sidestreet to the chandeliered Assembly Rooms on George Street in which half a dozen rooms of various size have been converted with lighting rigs and raked seating into theatres, reverts to its normal use, usually no use at all. Almost every available surface in August, from hoardings in front of shops either closed down or being refitted, to city-centre lamp-posts, is crazy-paved with posters advertising shows. In September, they're ripped down and the rain makes pulp out of what's left.

In Festival time the city, the Georgian grid of the New Town north of Waverley Station and the grey stone jumble of the Old Town south of it, is a log-jam of visitors from all across the globe, including theatre people here on business, seeing friends, shows, exhibitions, films, and concerts from early morning to early morning. For three weeks it is hard to believe this is a city that, on its ragged periphery, has council estates where some tenants live in darkness either because the electricity has been cut off or windows boarded up as the glass is repeatedly smashed by vandals; that Edinburgh is supposedly the AIDS capital of Europe; that Princes Street becomes during other months a night-time racing strip for black-leathered motorcyclists, their girls aimlessly eating take-away Wimpys and squatting on the backs of the memorial benches lining the railings of the gardens; that Lothian Road, where there are two five-star hotels, where world-acclaimed orchestras play at the Usher Hall, where the Film Festival overflows Filmhouse, is in winter a grotesque mile of neon-flashing pubs, Chinese and Italian take-aways, echoing to the sporadic violence of marauding teenage gangs on a night out, with their ear-rings, dyed hair and cheap chain-store fashions.

These are months when the Usher Hall is empty apart from the one night a week when the Scottish National Orchestra plays there and the audience darts quickly to their cars in the supervised multi-storey after a concert, when the Filmhouse audience scatters at the end of a film to the security of safer areas.

Edinburgh is grey stone-skirted and aloof, part of its disdain invested in the theory that England is the conspiring aggressor conducting some insidious and covert cultural invasion. Yet despite itself, it is becoming increasingly cosmopolitan. It is a small enough city to walk across, it is architecturally distinguished, a good city in which to live and work. And despite the Labour city council's political meddling in the Festival's affairs, Edinburgh in August is the focus of the arts world, with its world theatre season, its opera, its music, and its vast, sprawling Fringe.

Into this turbulent and unpredictable current, our adaptation of *The Grapes of Wrath* will drop, to scud wildly around, go under or float.

Monday 29   Looked for a second-hand paper-back of *The Grapes of Wrath* but finally bought a new copy, thus making a material commitment to the project and an investment in it of £2.95.

Read it once quickly at one sitting to refresh myself on narrative, again slowly for language, and again for themes and possible angles into adapting it.

It is even more theatrical than I remembered. The dialogue moves quickly with a muscular decisiveness and sings on the page. A studied, stylised language, formal yet colloquial, full of musicality, edged with grace notes, through which something direct and earthy suddenly springs. A unique rhythm, entirely unlike English cadences.

The Joads are not highly-educated people, not naturally verbally expressive. Tom Joad, despite being the leading character, is not linguistically articulate, although he is intelligent and thoughtful. Ma constantly asks for clarification, for explanations to be repeated, although her innate reasoning and forethought is acute. In fact, the only character to use language poetically, use image and metaphor, is the former preacher, Jim Casy.

But although the Joads and the migrant people are presented as naïve, they're in no way innocent. There is a major difference here. The Joads are bewildered by the world outside Sallisaw, Oklahoma, and have little grasp of its ways. They're appalled, uncomprehending, when they're tractored off their tenanted land, fleeced when they have to sell their belongings to raise the money to move. They allow themselves to be cajoled and bullied. All too often their explanation is that those harassing them 'ain' local'. So they're naïve in that sense. Yet they have a keen understanding of moral standards, codes of behaviour, worth, and decency. They are thoughtful, reflective. They are people of the land with a deep knowledge of the values and ways of nature. There is a strong sense in the book of the biological process, of conception, birth, youth, sex, ageing, and death, of natural harmony.

Portraying this difference between naïvety and innocence and its maturity into awareness and resolution will be difficult. The biggest problem in this context might well be Rose of Sharon, underwritten and, to me, the real failure in terms of character creation in the book.

There's a Biblical quality to Steinbeck's writing, reflecting the theme of parable, and which binds together the alternating chapters of the Joads' journey from dust-smothered Oklahoma to sun-baked California, with chapters of journalistic documentary of the times, politics (and some fairly tawdry political theorising by Steinbeck), and beautifully descriptive vignettes.

And the concept is Biblical, of course: the great exodus of a people from darkness to light, the migration to the so-called promised land, which turns out to be a hell. There's the echo of that disillusionment in Jim Casy, significantly a preacher no more.

The most important theme to me at the moment is faith. Its quality, its destruction, its resilience. 'You seem to have found a faith someplace alright,' says Pa to Ma near the end.

Two things I want to avoid. The overt religiosity in the texture of the book and in Casy. If I go for this too much, I'll be heading in the wrong direction, I think. Another is the politics. The novel has been seen as a pro-socialist piece (and as pro- and anti- a lot of other things as well, no doubt), but I don't think it is. What Steinbeck is saying is that mechanisation and commerce, instead of being the instrument of man has become his manager, driving the humanity and dignity from both 'sides' equally, from tenants and landlords, from workers and owners. It has become an external, abstract force. As the sharecropper says to the tenant he's tractoring off the land at the beginning of the book, 'Maybe the thing isn't men at all.'

Besides, I'm not interested in writing a political tract in the guise of a play. Leave that to others. I'm interested in feelings, nuances, crosscurrents, rhythms. Real drama.

Remember, I'm writing for a studio theatre. If Duncan can secure the Netherbow, as he hopes, the stage there is small: twenty feet by twenty feet. Also, this play must have a sensible running time, meaning less than two-and-a-half hours. With interval. So, I'm not writing a marathon, yet the script must do justice to the sweep of the novel. And to Steinbeck. And to the chance we have of doing it.

The novel falls naturally into two sections, two acts. First, the journey from Oklahoma to California (Steinbeck: 'The highway became their home and movement their means of expression'), the second, California itself, Hooverville, the government camp at Weedpatch, Hooper's Ranch, the boxcars, and, finally, the barn. Moving from aridity, dust, suffocation, to fertile land, water, giver and sustainer of life, and, lastly, the flood. A Biblical flood.

An odd thought – how, in old American films the rain is always intense, pounding back off the streets, not like English rain at all.

Possible colours for the set, if indeed there is one, or for lights: dull reds, ochres, colours of dust, rising to dazzling sunlight. Although a lot of the book takes place at night.

About the end: unsure about this at the moment. Tom leaves the book well before the final page, intent on following in Casy's footsteps. Ma, Pa, and Rose of Sharon remain to make their way to the barn where, finally, Rose of Sharon suckles the starving man. It's a madonna scene. Attacked by many critics as crude symbolism. Sloppy. Which in many ways it is and, unless I'm careful to avoid the religiosity of the book, something I'll only end up emphasising. Perhaps cut it altogether and end the play on Tom's exit?

If so, perhaps begin the play with Tom returning home, actually at the Joad household. It would make for dramatic symmetry, and cut the first eighty or so pages of the book, a great help when adapting a five-hundred-page novel into less than two-and-a-half hours' stage time.

My instinct is that the play should be rough-edged, raw, direct. Let the language weave an imaginative and imaginary fabric linking actors and audience. A lean, spare, dramatic style, a sparse, uncluttered stage, nothing getting in the way of the heart, the impulse. The actors an ensemble, creating momentum, velocity.

OCTOBER

Wednesday 1   Apparently, when John Ford's film of *The Grapes of Wrath* was released, it was considered suitable for showing in the Soviet Union, as the authorities thought it a devastating attack on capitalism. It was promptly withdrawn when it was discovered that, whatever the iniquities of the West, Russian audiences envied the fact that every proletarian American family appeared to own a car.

Thursday 2   Preliminary research: re-reading *The Grapes of Wrath*, of course, plus some earlier novels, *Tortilla Flat*, *Of Mice and Men*, *The Long Valley*; and a couple of later ones, *Cannery Row*, *East of Eden*; Malcolm Bradbury's *The Modern American Novel*, Warren French's study of Steinbeck, Studs Terkel's *Hard Times* and the Steinbeck letters. This, from 1933: 'The fascinating thing to me is the way the group has a soul, a drive, an intent, a method, a reaction and a set of tropisms which in no way resemble the same things possessed by the men who make up the group.'

This is reflected clearly in the individual characters and their relation to the larger migrant group in the novel. But the group theme in the novel, described in the journalistic chapters that alternate with those telling the fictional story of the Joads, is something I don't want to lose sight of in the play. On a basic level, there's an immediate dramatic choice: to pinpoint the Joads, show their experiences and each separate character reaching his or her individual resolution and merely make reference to the wider world of a nation on the move; or to go the other way, write that nation and show the Joads as incidental instruments of it. Or try some combination.

It looks as though the centre of the play will not be Tom Joad, but Tom and Casy – through them the two worlds can be brought into play, through Casy's idea of 'everybody being part of one big soul'. But a point to watch here is that Casy doesn't become a bore because he's the sort of man who does the right thing for the right reason. As Tom's violence makes him interesting, so Casy must have his complexity, his mystery, as well. One thing I am determined to do is not get into the commonly held view that Jim Casy is a symbol of Jesus Christ because he has been in the wilderness, speaks a similar line before he is killed, and even has the same initials. In fact I want to avoid the religiosity of the book, as religiosity, as much as possible. Think of it as a much wider thing, a spiritual seam crushed between other seams, each of them with their own richness.

One of the things that does interest me is the journey aspect. All fiction, all drama, is a form of journey; someone or some group moving, not necessarily geographically, but intellectually and emotionally across an individual or several terrains, arriving at a point of resolution or defeat, either by their own will or that of others. Chekhov was a master of this: look at *Uncle Vanya*, *The Cherry Orchard*. *Grapes*, of course, has a strong journeying and mythical dimension (Steinbeck: 'It's a form of fantasy').

In fact, there are two great American myths at work in this novel: the American notion of westering, and a kind of heroic evolution, man's journey from solitude and darkness to potential fulfilment in freedom and light. The twist in the novel is that it is these very myths which are corrupt, which rot and decay like the fruit on the Californian ranches. What Steinbeck does is simultaneously to celebrate and shatter the American Dream.

So, is it an optimistic novel, and will it be an optimistic play? I think it is, and what happens on stage must be seen as capable of being interpreted in an optimistic light.

Warren French calls this process, whereby each character reaches a personal resolution, 'the education of the heart', and draws parallels with Dickens' *Hard Times*. I'd add, too, *Nicholas Nickleby*. One of the things that David Edgar did in that dramatisation was, by having Nicholas clutch the dead Smike to him in the final Christmas scene, and punch his fist in the air, was to make the point, derived from the novel, that although the actual story of what happens to the characters is ended, the book, and the conditions it describes, is actually unfinished, sociologically incomplete. Steinbeck is exactly the same. Tom and Rose reach their personal resolutions at the end of the novel about fifty pages apart. If I can find some way of actually bringing them together on stage, it will hopefully make the complete–incomplete point, and, if I'm careful, avoid the sentimentality of Steinbeck's ending. I also like the notion of brother and sister being together in stage image but separate in time and space.

Steinbeck's alternating chapters, moving from the general to the particular, prompts the idea of using a narrator for the play. Problem – who, exactly, is the narrator? One of the Joads, who moves in and out of character? Or Casy? If so, how do I make it clear he is, when he's narrating, no longer the character he is at other times? And will it be 'general' if the audience identifies that actor with 'personal'? Should, then, a narrator be permanently at the side of the stage, playing no other part? And, if so, the same question, who is he? Steinbeck himself, perhaps? This might work ... Steinbeck as narrator would come between the audience and the Joads, creating a distancing effect helping the audience to see the other characters as representatives of a nation of migrant people, helping to create that slightly de-personalising 'form of fantasy' ...

If I start with the narrator telling the story of the dustbowl and the Depression, do I have to end with him?

Should the 'Battle Hymn of the Republic' come in somewhere? Steinbeck insisted it be published in the first US edition of the novel, but I believe the publishers were none too happy and printed it at the back. As far as I know, it's been dropped from every other edition. Should I reinstate it somehow?

Saturday 4   Meeting with Duncan.
Confirm that we're setting the play firmly in the period and time scale of the book.

The thing is, Steinbeck is vague about period. Although it is obviously the mid-1930s, nowhere is there mention of a particular year in which the events take place. Drought and dust destroyed sweeps of southern and mid-western farmland in 1934, migrants were travelling westward in 1935, and Steinbeck himself made the journey in 1937. And it is actually quite difficult clearly tracing the Joad story in terms of months and seasons. I plan to work through this, perhaps making a wallchart.

Agree on the two-act structure of the play. He knocks on the head my idea of using a narrator, and especially using Steinbeck as a narrator, his point being that as much as possible should be integrated into dialogue and action. He's quite right.

He suggests using slides of photographs of the period projected onto a backcloth either at the rear or side of the stage. My turn to reject. I don't believe the transition from live experience to two-dimensional image works in the theatre. Whenever I've seen it done it looks like a bad compromise.

As to the set, neither of us wants to use a truck, or at least some sort of vehicle, or trolley, with wheels, making turns around the stage. This is liberating both dramatically and technically. Although the whole of Act One will centre on travel, the Joads lead a make-do, precarious life, and to imagine the truck directly reflects this. And, as Jonathan Miller says in *Subsequent Performances*, it is invariably true that nature looks atrocious on stage – if we can think of a truck as nature for a moment.

Instead, we'll go for a few old wooden boxes, a couple of blankets, tarpaulins, the essence of the archaeology and spirit of the novel, the actors improvising. As bare a stage as possible will make things more spontaneous, expressionist, concentrating everything on simplicity, language, and acting.

Characters: obviously we can't even if we wanted to, use all in the book, even all the Joads. I want to use whatever characters carry and focus the themes most clearly. Agree to cut Muley Graves, whom Tom and Casy meet in Sallisaw at the beginning and who stays there; Uncle John, Pa's brother, a morbid, background figure, intermittent drunk who still believes he contributed to his wife's death (the guilt theme, if I decide to use it, is better rooted in Pa, who blames himself for Noah's condition because he grasped his son's skull as he was being born). We cut the children, Ruthie and Winfield, for practical as much as dramatic reasons. Ditto the dog. Cutting Ruthie means her betrayal of Tom, telling someone that he killed the guard who kills Casy, has to be reassigned to another character. It will also mean it changes from an unintentional to an intentional betrayal. Maybe Rose of Sharon betrays Tom? Does she do it intentionally?

Arrive at a cast list of Ma, Pa, Tom, Al, Rose of Sharon, Connie Rivers, Jim Casy. This also cuts Grampa, Granma, and Noah. Although I feel we might need Noah. There will be smaller parts, pickets, migrant workers at the camps, the starving man in the barn, and as both Connie and Noah leave the Joads about half-way through, we could use those actors for other roles, as I'd rather the actors playing main parts stay with them all the way through. On the whole, it's probably better to start off this way and add, rather than desperately reducing later on. Which I'll probably end up doing, anyway.

On an administrative note, Duncan has secured the afternoon slot at the Netherbow for the Fringe, so another problem, the all-important one of venue, looks solved. On the Fringe you have a flying start by being in the Assembly Rooms or the Traverse Theatre, a good start by being in the Netherbow on the High Street or Richard Demarco's round the corner in Blackfriars Street, and you're in with a chance if you're near the Assembly Rooms. Anywhere else and you're relying solely on your advertising because audiences and critics are conservative, they check what's on at the known venues first.

He will also telephone Adline Finlay and Hal Easton to tell them work has begun.

Monday 6   Trace the Joads' route in *The Times Concise Atlas of the World*. Sallisaw lies almost 160 miles east of Oklahoma City, near the crook of a river flowing south-east and eventually into the Mississippi. The nearest town of any importance, judging from the size of the typeface, is Fort Smith. From Sallisaw a thin red line meanders westwards across the map through places familiar from the novel: Gore, Warner, Checotah, Henrietta, Castle, Paden, where the Joads fill up the tank of the Hudson with petrol. Then on through Oklahoma City. From there, out on to Highway 66, the great concrete artery that snakes across the south-west from the Mississippi to California. At Bethany, they stop for the night beside the road, meet Ivy and Sairy Wilson from Kansas, themselves California-bound. Here Grampa Joad dies, and the remaining Joads and Wilsons decide to divide their loads equally between their two trucks and forge on together. On to Texola and the state line into Texas, through the Panhandle, through Amarillo. To the north-west is Pampa, the home of the man they later meet at Needles. Days and nights on the road. Driving, driving. Living rough. On through Glenrio and the state line into New Mexico. Along by the Pecos River, crossing at Santa Rosa. Here, Rose of Sharon tells Ma that, once in California, Connie has ideas of studying at home, of buying a store, and that Tom and Al could work for him. Their baby might even be born in a hospital. Soon the Wilsons' car breaks down again. Tom suggests he and Casy repair it while the others drive on. Ma stages her first act of defiance. Weighing a jack-handle in her hand, she threatens violence if the family separates. Pa, the decision-maker, is astonished. Tom placates her. Highway 66 on and into Arizona, high into the mountains at Flagstaff. Dry, rocky land at Oatman, then Topock, crossing the Colorado River and the state line into California. But so near and yet so far. Over 300 miles of ochre Mojave Desert lie before them. They stop on the west side of the river at Needles. Tom and Pa meet the Texan on his way home; they first hear from him the word 'Okies'. Here, too, Noah tells Tom he's leaving the family to live by the river. The Wilsons also stay behind, Sairy too ill to travel. Then the long haul across the desert, starting early afternoon, breaking the back of it at night. Secluded high on the back of the truck, Rose of Sharon and Connie silently make love. A stop at the inspection point at Daggett, and by dawn the Hudson lumbers into Techachapi and the Joads at last see the green valleys of California below. Journey's end. Ma reveals her secret: Granma, old, weary, and sick, died during the night.

On the other side of Bakersfield, the destination of hundreds of thousands of migrants swamping California, is the Hooverville squatter camp where the Joads meet Floyd Knowles, six months searching for work, where Casy allows himself to be arrested after Floyd assaults a deputy, and Connie runs off before the camp is burned. South along Highway 99, the Joads' next port of call, the government camp at Weedpatch. There the Wallace father and son find Tom a day's work laying drainage pipes on Mr Thomas's ranch. Thomas tells them cops have bribed men to start a fight at the camp's dance so they can get a warrant for the migrants' eviction. Tom, Al, and others prevent the fight taking place, but the Joads fail to find work. Ma decides they must leave. Back they drive through Bakersfield, past the rebuilt Hooverville, north to Pixley, then east where they are run in with a convoy of others to Hooper's Ranch. Here, the peach-pickers are herded by the family into dark, one-roomed huts. Armed guards patrol day and night. Illegally slipping under the wire fence, Tom meets Casy, who has joined a picket against low wages. They are ambushed, Tom kills the guard who murders Casy. Again, Ma plans their strategy. They drive northwards again. Rose of Sharon's pregnancy is well advanced, the family spirit is derelict. Finally they reach the cotton fields, the boxcars and the barn.

I make a wallchart of the places and events and, as far as possible, mark in the appropriate months, beginning in summer, ending the following spring.

NOVEMBER

Wednesday 19   First diary entry for six weeks – the
reason being that work has started. My desk has become the scene of a
tide of paper washing, usually confoundingly, via the typewriter,
in the form of try-outs, lines of dialogue, ideas, continuity suggestions,
parts of entire sequences, from a stack of A4 pads to the waste-
paper basket. Surfacing somehow amid the wreckage, Act One, draft
one.

As bits and pieces have floated up, I've netted them and taken them
round to Duncan at weekends, rather like a student taking a continuous
assessment thesis to his professor. Duncan reads it, marking the stuff, as
it were, while I silently study the weave of the carpet or the tree outside
the window. So the weeks have passed, Duncan, me, the carpet, the tree.

But, a draft. Something you can pick up, weigh. Something which
might not be, even at this stage, as healthy as it could be, but, at least, in the
world.

In fact, too much of it is in the world. It's an enormous 73 pages long.
The cast list has expanded, too. Apart from Ma, Pa, Tom, Al, Rose of
Sharon, Connie, and Casy, there is Grampa, Ivy Wilson, Sairy Wilson,
and a group at the beginning: a tenant, a landowner, another tenant,
the sharecropper paid to tractor others off the land, a used-car salesman
– the economic background. Added to these are the petrol attendant at
Paden, the one-eyed manager of the wrecking yard, and the Texan at
Needles.

And I still haven't written Scene One. I have the idea of the play
opening in the executive office of a New York bank. Someone tracing his
finger down graphs of crop yield, profits, the faceless bureaucrat
abstractly ruining lives far away, someone more interested in going to
the movies that night ... A man sitting at a desk, his secretary
somewhere to the side, a venetian blind over a rear window. An Edward
Hopper scene. But it's not working out.

Really, this draft and the sketch plan I have for Act Two, is nothing
more than an organisation of pieces from the book in which Casy has
become the narrator and central character until, in Act Two, Tom
inherits the baton after Casy's death. I am, though, pleased with some of
the transitions from scene to scene. The effect I'm aiming for is the
cinematic cut. An example: Tom, just released from prison, meets Casy
on the road. They talk. Ma emerges into the acting area: 'Oh, Tommy,

thank God', and we're into the next scene. Seamlessly, I hope.

Wednesday 26   Stratford: Vivien and I take a five-day break in Stratford, staying at a small b&b run by a jovial, apple-faced Major, a retired rep for a brewery, and his deferential, stick-like wife.

To *The Rover*, Aphra Behn's 1677 play, set in a Spanish colony during carnival. Well-to-do girls disguise themselves to look for husbands, Englishmen are out on the razzle, a country squire is duped by a whore and her boyfriend, and a celebrated courtesan falls in love with the eponymous buccaneering rover. As the stage at The Swan is open on three sides, the set is minimal, almost the only prop being a good-sized flat-topped wooden chest, of the type in which linen used to be stored. This might be a good idea for *Grapes*. A wooden chest for our play would symbolise domesticity, frugality. It can be sat on for the truck, rooted inside for the car wrecking-yard scene, used as desk, bed, table, section of hut, boxcar. And, as in *The Rover*, it is improvisational, actorly.

The Rover moves instantly from location to location on lighting cues. It doesn't matter if the audience don't immediately know where they are, as they accept the convention that this is a fast, flowing arena show. The roistering spirit of the piece is far more important than names and places. Besides the plot is far too complicated to worry about following every detail. But the point is, you don't have to spell everything out and underline it.

Sunday 30   Stratford: to The Other Place, for a lecture by Barry Kyle on his main house production of *Richard II*. The attitudes to kingship embodied by Richard and the pretender Boling-broke he sees as pinpointing a fundamental crisis: who owns the Garden of England? This became his central, or one of his central, themes, reflected in the production design of a series of garden landscapes with a wrought-iron arc, representing a section of clockface, like a rainbow over the stage.

This is applicable to *The Grapes*. One of the strongest threads running through its increasingly textured cloth is the conflict between worker and owner, the possessing and the dispossessed. With its subsidiary strands of the conflict between man and the inexorable machine of commerce, and between man and nature itself, it is, in essence, the conflict of who owns the Garden.

Meanwhile, the Major appears out to prove that if anyone now owns the Garden of England, or at any rate that part of it in the West Midlands, it is him. Every spare moment he regales us with the kind of elaborate, possibly exaggerated, vastly entertaining monologues he must have once, and undoubtedly still does, regale them with in the saloon bar. How, when his vacuum cleaner broke down and the local reps 'infesting Coventry' proved incompetent, he telephoned, reversing the charges, to the chairman of the company in America to complain. How, again to complain, he talked his way into the area manager's office of some nationalised industry by telling the secretary he was the manager's cousin, hadn't seen him for ages, just passing, want to surprise him, why don't I take in the morning coffee? Afterwards he sent her a box of chocolates. Getting one over on officials is his glorious, anarchic campaign of life. Anyone who 'likes a drink' wins his approval; anyone who doesn't is thereby a somewhat dubious character. Thus Montgomery. Once, during the war, the Major, Montgomery, and other 'brass' watched the field test of an amphibious vehicle in the grounds of Jeffrey Amherst's estate ('One of Noel Coward's friends'; this with a conspiratorial wink and a nudging elbow movement). The vehicle approached the lake, entered the water and promptly sank, causing laughter to all but Montgomery. 'Of course, he never really liked a drink, you know.' The Major's opinion is that Britain won the war with luck but little judgement, infiltrated as we were by teetotallers.

DECEMBER

Sunday 7   Real difficulties with Act Two,
which must be finished by Christmas. It's naturally far more static than
Act One, focusing not on travel but place. Or rather, five places:
Hooverville, Weedpatch, Hooper's Ranch, the boxcars and the barn,
and the problem is achieving a sense of momentum so that it builds
dramatically to the flood and Rose of Sharon giving birth to her dead
child, a sequence which I'm delaying writing. Fright, probably.

I have not moved Ruthie's betrayal of Tom from its place in the novel,
the boxcars, but reassigned it to Rose of Sharon. I think she bears a
resentment against Tom because it is for his benefit as much as the
search for work that the family move from one place to another in
California. She possibly, in some sense, blames him for Connie's
desertion. And, as her labour approaches, and as she is not getting the
food or milk she should, distrust and anger ferment within her, culmi-
nating in her offstage betrayal which she then confesses to Ma.

This will entail my going back to the beginning and re-writing Rose
and Connie, discovering an understanding, or lack of it, between
Connie and Tom, and substantiating Rose to give her enough emotional
and psychological impetus. This is the kind of reconstruction work by
which the play will hopefully become a different entity from the book,
take on its own form, breathe its own air, live its own life.

For the first time, two entirely invented characters have made their
entrance. Well, that's not strictly accurate. They appear in the book,
fleetingly, as the un-named contractor and the Deputy Sheriff (who
answers to both Joe and Mike) at Hooverville. I've just extended them,
pushed them centre stage, given them names. Persky and Bird. Why
Persky and Bird, I haven't a clue. Sounds like a vaudeville double-act,
although I'm sure I've never read or heard of one called that.

Persky is emblematic, a ranch-owner, a hard-nosed, persuasive local
politician, an amalgam of the attitudes most Californians have towards
the 'Okies'. He appears at the top of Act Two, introduced by
community-minded Sheriff Bird, giving a speech to the Bakersfield
Association in his capacity as Chairman of the Public Health Committee. He is smiling, placatory, liberal. He is aware of the hostility against
the 'Okies' from some quarters but, rest assured, the Committee is
doing everything possible for them, providing health care and sanitation at
Hooverville. Lies, of course, immediately exposed in a speech describ-

ing the real conditions at the camp by Floyd Knowles, squatting amid dereliction at the other side of the stage. And by Persky himself, who appears at Hooverville wearing his other hat (though not, I trust, literally). He has contracted more land and is recruiting peach-pickers to work it. Bird, his good nature left behind in Bakersfield, threatens the burning of the camp if the migrants don't pack up and go. Later, Persky will print more leaflets urging workers to come to California and once more drop the wages on his peach farms. So the cycle will go on.

The aim is that Persky and Bird will work dramatically in a similar way to the tenant/used-car salesman sequence in Act One. But, as with Act One, for the present it's just far too long.

Completed Act One, draft two. Cut down to 58 pages, still too long, but at least going in the right direction. And I have managed to write, or collate from the effluent of rejects, a draft of Act One, Scene One. The one set in the New York bank. Not worth detailing, as I suspect its presence in the play will be temporary. Probably only an overnight visit.

Sunday 14   Act Two, draft one completed.
Typed out END OF PLAY for the first time. Dispiritingly, 67 pages, making the whole draft 125 pages long. The schedule at the theatre at the moment is that a one-man Beckett show is due to follow us at 5pm; if anyone performs this draft they'll have to play Act One one day and Act Two the next. Again, Act Two has an expanded cast list, with Persky and Bird, pickets, the Wainwrights who live in one section of the boxcar, and the starving man in the barn. Everything has to be cut. And it's not a process of hacking stuff out; it's working from base upwards.

The ending is a failure, pretty much as it is in the book. Tom exits as in the novel, the family struggle on alone through the flood, the stillbirth and the barn. Dramatically, it's dismal, precisely the double ending the novel is accused of having. I can't think why I didn't (a) choose my first option and end it on Tom's exit, or (b) go for my second and try to bring brother and sister thematically together somehow. Seduced by those three words, I suppose, END OF PLAY.

Back to the beginning . . .

1987

JANUARY

Monday 5   Sudden panic. Duncan has seen
Hal Easton, over here to make preliminary Festival arrangements, and
reports that he has given him a draft script to take back to America. This
is staggering. I had hoped to nurture it, coax it, make it ready for the
world (re-write the thing), in solitary peace for a little while longer. I take
him blow by blow through its handing over. Duncan confirms that it
goes to New York as an exploratory text; a lot of things we want to work
on, points to emerge, things to edit out, nothing at all fixed as yet, still
discovering character and language, etc. – in fact, as encrusted with
provisos as an old suitcase is with destination labels.

The plan is that Hal is to show the script to Rob Mulholland, Studio's
artistic director. Rob, he says, 'is marvellous at seeing potential. One of
his directorial fortes is ensemble theatre.' Pointed out that he would
have to examine it forensically for any evidence of potential or ensemble.
Accused of being a pessimist.

At any rate, Rob will telephone his reactions by 13 February.

On the script itself, Duncan suggests breaking up Casy's wodges of
Act One narration by both cutting and distributing parts to other
characters. This makes sense but at the same time diffuses the idea of
emphasising the fact that although Casy travels with the Joads, he is
himself neither a Joad nor a sharecropper, that he is going to California
for other reasons, to put the theories he has developed to practical use.

Duncan's argument is that this is self-evident and doesn't need
emphasising at all – that narration must also be from the perspectives of
others as common experiences on the road will be interpreted by
individuals according to their own values, so telling us a lot more about
each character. There is, he points out, almost no narration in Act
Two, apart from the picket line outside Hooper's Ranch, when Casy
steps from the crowd and tells us what's happened to him since we saw
him last, being arrested at Hooverville. Therefore, there is a severe
imbalance in the play's dynamic that cutting and redistribution will help
correct – and hopefully help find the ensemble we're striving for.

Act One, Scene One, he says, has to go. Ripping it from its staples and dropping it over the arm of his chair, he begins a line by line examination of Scene Two. I crawl about the floor retrieving my three typed sheets, wondering what his reaction would be if I said I thought it should stay. Which I don't, of course. I'm glad to be shot of it. I've learned that if something feels wrong, it's because it is wrong. And the bank president scene felt like a clamp over my windpipe.

I'm discovering that Duncan has a very good stage eye, an instinct about what will read in practical terms and what will not. His solutions to problems of staging, after several moments of impenetrable silence, gazing at the wall, often appear so logically simple that I find myself mildly miffed at not having been able to think of them myself. But it's a directness that has come from a long experience of stage management and working on shows, at Birmingham Rep and in the West End, experience I don't have. Then it strikes me that if the answers are comparatively simple, is the play, my writing, simplistic? No, this is ridiculous. Open the door and the doubts tumble in like a gang of jabbering acrobats.

He is prodding the buttons of his calculator, estimating how much it would cost us to produce the play ourselves. To hire the theatre for three weeks, pay for publicity, using the minimum number of British actors we could get away with, even at this stage involving a radical re-think of the whole concept of the play, and assuming nobody gets paid (payment is rare on the Fringe), would cost us at the very least, £5,000. Which, he says, is out of the question. I immediately, enthusiastically agree. We are in the hands of Studio Productions. Silence again. The tree outside the window, I notice, seems devoid of life.

Later: just checked – 13 February is both a Friday and a full moon.

Tuesday 6   There were a couple of other news items yesterday I didn't bother to record last night.

Both Hal and Rob are 'interested' in *The Grapes*. (That word, of course, covers every conceivable eventuality.) More concretely encouraging is that if they accept the play, they will pay all its production costs. The company will come to Edinburgh for seven weeks, four to rehearse, three to perform. Hal and Rob will be visiting a couple of times before this to finalise administration. And they are keen on producing a large-cast show. We are thinking provisionally of a cast of ten, large by our standards, and they haven't balked at that. So, we estimate the possibility of *The Grapes* being produced by Studio as being somewhere between a cautious 'perhaps' and a possible 'maybe'. There is still this little matter of the script being approved by the Estate, of course . . .

Thursday 22   London: in London to record interviews for a radio documentary I'm both writing and presenting on the work of opera director Graham Vick. Tonight to the National Theatre, to see *Three Men on a Horse*, the John Cecil Holm and George Abbott comedy directed by Jonathan Lynn at the Cottesloe. The play itself is slight: timid little Erwin Trowbridge of New Jersey writes four-line verses for greetings cards, but has an unerring knack of picking the winners in horse races. He never bets as this would spoil the fun of marking his tips in the morning paper on the bus into work, and checking them off in the evening paper on the bus home, copying the results in a notebook. Crisis when his wife finds the book and concludes that the names and digits are chorus girls and their phone numbers. In drunk despair at a New York hotel, Erwin falls in with three professional gamblers who discover his talent and put him to work making money. He also finds himself involved with a hoodlum's moll.

But the revelation to me is that the play is set in 1935, the year the mid-western dust-storms were at their most intense, when two million tenant farmers were heading west. In 1935 America was in the trough of the Depression: five thousand banks had closed in the three years following the Wall Street Crash in 1929 and millions lost all their savings. In 1933 Roosevelt won the Presidency on a New Deal ticket, although the Depression only really came to an end with increased defence spending in 1939.

But seeing the play made me think about how much theatre, and film, popular song, and, in its time, vaudeville, like music hall in this country, dealt with contemporary catastrophe by interpreting it as the basis for comedy. For what this play is saying is, first, what a bewitching but daft commodity money is, and second, that personal happiness is something entirely independent of it. What shows like this must have done, and it was a great hit when first produced, was console with humour, uniting people by making fun out of what was causing their troubles. Hart and Kaufman's *You Can't Take It With You* must have worked in the same way a year later, in 1936. Broadway musicals and Busby Berkeley films served a similar purpose by creating an alternative world for a couple of hours, glittering, glamorous, cellophane-wrapped against the great drudgery outside, in which lines, loops, and wheels of girls high-kicked in synchronised extravaganzas across stages and up and down long curving staircases, dancing, dancing, dancing . . .

I decide to set *The Grapes* in 1935. It would be interesting as well to see if there's any room in it for a glimpse, perhaps an ironic glimpse, of that antidote world. Perhaps by radio . . .

I'm writing this in the airless mega-heat of my hotel room. The choice is between overnight suffocation, or opening the double glazing and the windows to the banshee wailings and lunatic howlings from Villiers Street below.

Friday 23　　　　　　　　　　　Slept intermittently last night with windows closed and a wet face-cloth over forehead, like some crude pastiche of a film-star. First thing this morning, to a chemist on the Strand to buy toothpaste. Queued behind three bruised and silent dossers being given free glasses of pink antiseptic mouthwash by an earnest-looking pharmacist.

FEBRUARY

Tuesday 3   A letter from Studio Productions, its import summed up in four words near the end, a dash of American pizzazz which Duncan and I unashamedly savour: 'Let's make it happen.'

Immediately I look upon the detritus covering my desk, from which the typewriter appears like a monolith, not as the strewn rubble of the present draft but as the productive working quarry of the next.

It's an enormous boost. Actually having a date by which the draft would be read is a rare courtesy indeed, but beating their own deadline shows these people can do their stuff. I guess it's what the Americans call 'attitude'. The fact that Studio want to take the project further, and write so eloquently, and at reassuring length, about the draft, its selection of themes, its characterisation, potential, and their judicious use of words like 'visceral' to describe the text, colours my assessment of them no end, of course.

Monday 23   Over the past few weeks, God knows how many re-writes, additions, discardings of how many sections. Another draft completed, copies of which are going to Hal, and Adline Finlay at the English Theatre Guild. For the sake of clarity, it's being dubbed *Grapes One*.

The running order of the script at this stage is as follows: Act One, Scene One – tenants, owners, Joe Davis's son, and the Used-Car Salesman, based on Chapters 2, 5, and 7; Scene Two – Tom, returning from McAlester Jail, meeting Casy on the road (Chapter 4); Scene Three – Tom's homecoming, meeting the family again, Ma's news that Granma has died (Chapters 8 and 10); Scene Four – the Joads, having sold their possessions, decide when to leave (Chapter 10); Scene Five – packing and leaving (Chapter 10); Scene Six – the road next day, meeting the Wilsons and the death of Grampa (Chapters 10 and 13); Scene Seven – the road again, the petrol station incident (Chapter 13); Scene Eight – the road, Rose of Sharon's and Connie's plans for buying a store in California, Ma's rebellion when the Wilsons' truck breaks down (Chapter 16); Scene Nine – the car wrecking-yard and the manager, One-Eye (Chapter 16); Scene Ten – the Colorado River bank (Chapter 18); Scene Eleven – Sairy Wilson's memories of her childhood and the Joads leaving to cross the Mojave Desert alone (Chapter 18); Scene Twelve – driving through Mojave and the first sight of the valleys of California (Chapter 18).

Act Two, Scene One – the meeting of the Bakersfield Association, Floyd Knowles, Persky recruiting men, and the arrest of Casy (Chapter 20); Scene Two – Weedpatch Government Camp (Chapter 22); Scene Three – Weedpatch, preparing for the dance (Chapter 24); Scene Four – Tom, Al, and a man who tries to break up the dance, whom I've christened Higgins (Chapter 24); Scene Five – Ma's decision the Joads should leave Weedpatch (Chapter 26); Scene Six – Casy on the picket line outside Hooper's Ranch (Chapters 25 and 26); Scene Seven – the Joads at Hooper's Ranch (Chapter 26); Scene Eight – Tom meeting Casy outside Hooper's, murder of Casy, murder of guard (Chapter 26); Scene Nine – Hooper's Ranch: Rose of Sharon accusing Tom of killing again, Ma's decision the Joads should leave (Chapter 26); Scene Ten – the road from Hooper's to the boxcars (Chapter 26); Scene Eleven – the boxcar, the Wainwrights, Rose of Sharon's confession to Ma she has betrayed Tom (Chapter 28); Scene Twelve – the culvert where Tom is hiding, Ma and Tom's last meeting (Chapter 28); Scene Thirteen – the boxcar, Al's plans of marriage to Aggie Wainwright, the rains, the building of the bank that fails to stop the flood, Rose of Sharon's labour and stillbirth (Chapter 30); Scene Fourteen – the boxcar, the aftermath (Chapter 30); Scene Fifteen – the barn (Chapter 30). Still 125 pages long.

This is the broadest, most basic outline, the most significant contours of the map. There are more subtle features on the terrain, dips, slopes, and ridges, strata of rock and clay. Ideas and dialogue transposed from earlier parts of the novel to later parts of the play, and vice versa, to focus a theme or a moment more clearly, or substantiate the dramatic impulse of a scene or character.

It's important, for instance, that only Casy, and not Pa and Tom as well, talk at the Colorado River with the Texan who warns there is no work in California and that all the land is owned by giant corporations, confirming Casy's unspoken fears. I want Pa to carry the illusion of the good life in California the furthest, and for it not to be broken until, and by, California itself; for his loss of hope to be set alongside Ma's finding faith and trust that they will somehow survive, and his abdication as head of the family to coincide with Ma's assumption of the decision-making process.

Also, Act One must establish the Tom–Casy bond; they must have time together where Casy expounds his observations and theories and

35

Tom stops shrugging them off and begins to absorb. Tom's only contact with anyone outside the family and Casy in Act One is with the Wilsons, the petrol attendant, and One-Eye, the last two both aggressive and bitter and with whom Tom fails to reason and threatens violence. It is from Casy that I want Tom to be seen learning the art and heart of reason. From his own experiences in California, Tom will come to understand the absent Casy, judge for himself that he was right, and become his successor. For the same reason, Floyd's description of Hooverville at the top of Act Two is made directly to the audience as a counterpoint to Persky and not, as in the book, to Tom and Al.

Tom and Ma operate a little differently. When the travellers first see the valleys in Act One, Scene Twelve, nobody actually mentions the word 'California' until Tom speaks the penultimate line helping Ma down from the truck: 'We're there, Ma. California.'

Ma: 'Thank God. Oh, thank God. The family's here.' The trip word, 'California', reflects back to their earlier exchange in Sallisaw, in which Ma expresses her suspicions of the promises of the west: 'I'm a-scared o' stuff so nice. Maybe somepin ain't so nice about it.'

Then, Tom replies that he learned one lesson in prison – you can't think ahead to the day you're going to be released: 'You just gotta take ever' day as she comes'. It is a line Ma will repeat to Pa in Act Two, Scene Fourteen.

Pa, disillusioned and broken, says it seems as though everything is over. They're beaten.

Ma says they'll carry on.

'Well, you seemed to have found a faith someplace, alright,' says Pa.

'Somepin Tommy tol' me,' she replies. 'You just gotta take ever' day as she comes.' There is a special union between Ma and her second eldest son. Sometimes she sees him almost as a visionary.

So, each character in this draft is finding their own definition of faith and responsibility, their own resolution. Ma, the tough, able, but subservient provider of food by which the family is supported, becomes the source of a greater nourishment, a rock-like presence of emotional and spiritual strength against which the family shelters. Tom inherits Casy's mantle. There is the flicker (only a flicker at the moment) of Rose of Sharon's growth from pampered child-wife, buffeting about on her sea of despair after Connie leaves, wracked by hysteria, emerging almost as a second, younger Ma, a woman sustaining life, suckling the dying man. Ma, Tom, Rose of Sharon are united in that each find peace and purpose.

Perhaps something could be made of Al's intention to marry Aggie Wainwright, whom, incidentally, we never see. Will the marriage work out, I wonder? Pa fades into failure. And fades in the script, as well. Problems ahead, but I think it's on the right lines. It's pretty relentless. And not nearly enough a play in its own right. But a basis for one. Re-writing Rose of Sharon and Connie might help a bit of sharpening up all round.

Should record the excision of Adams. Another invented character, Adams appeared, briefly, as did Persky and Bird in a scene in the Deputy's Bakersfield office, in Act Two between what are now Scenes Two and Three. He (Adams) was a newspaper man, his copy vetted by, and usually written at the instigation of, Persky and Bird.

In the novel, Tom meets the Wallace father and son at Weedpatch, who introduce him to the man they work for, Mr Thomas, who takes Tom on. Because of a grudge he has against the Farmers' Association, and because he is sympathetic to the migrants, he tells them the cops plan to raid the Weedpatch dance. Because they can only enter a government camp with a warrant, men have been bribed to start a fight while the dance is in progress.

Rather than have my cumbersome Wallace–Thomas–Tom try-out in the script, I created a short scene in which Persky and Bird are discussing with Adams, in appropriately ambiguous language, over a couple of drinks, the efficacy of such a raid should one prove necessary. Adams is amenable to producing a Bird-approved report, subject to his usual consideration. What this scene intended to show was the complicity of the police, politicians, landowners, and the Press. Thomas's information is (and still is), reported by Tom to the family in the following scene.

Duncan and I discussed this. I rather liked Adams, but began to see that nothing would be lost by killing him off. Agreed to do so. But the complicity idea might be useful if we need it.

MARCH

Thursday 5   Rob Mulholland and Albert Bennett, artistic director and dramaturg of Studio Productions, are flying to Edinburgh on 18 March for a week of script discussions. A week? What is so wrong that will take a week to sort out? On the other hand, looking on the bright side, two people aren't going to fly across the Atlantic to discuss the script for any length of time if they're not actually interested in producing it.

Wednesday 11   Read an article by Christopher Hampton from the *Guardian* of January 1986, about his adaptation of Choderlos de Laclos' *Les Liaisons Dangereuses*. His first problem was to find a language appropriate both to the novel's period (eighteenth century), and epistolary form: 'At the third attempt I hit a note which I then made every effort to sustain, a kind of language, artificial but tied to no period, elaborate but direct, the object of which was to mirror the novel's difficult combination of scientific detachment and perilous emotional extremes. This solution had the added advantage of being sufficiently flexible to accommodate the differences in tone between the various characters so carefully established by Laclos; because although the characters may not speak much dialogue, they are all given distinct voices.'

Christopher Hampton is one of the finest adaptors and playwrights. *Les Liaisons* achieves superbly what every adaptation should, it stands as a brilliant play entirely in its own right.

Language, in fact, has been my major problem, but so far an intensely enjoyable one. I am English, so is Duncan. The American language is something that, spoken, has come to us primarily from films. Steinbeck's language is, therefore, not something I am familiar with although, of course, with the exception of a few expressions, I understand it, and those few expressions are clear enough in their context. But 'clear enough' is obviously insufficient to work with, and even the most apparently accessible dialogue takes on a certain opacity when its rhythms and nuances are not naturally your own.

I treated it, still do, as something entirely new. As American, not English. I let its cadences, its musicality be my principal guide. I read it aloud constantly, searching for the rhythmic through-line, especially in the words, lines, passages in the script which are not Steinbeck, but written by me. These are the big danger areas, for although I've attempted absolute integration, it's easy to go wrong. But at least I have the safety net of its being read carefully by Americans.

Another part of the language problem is that the Joads are not themselves (unlike Steinbeck), verbally expansive. So, in writing new material for them, I have to watch for consistency, choosing a vocabulary that is not necessarily expressive in itself, but using words which hopefully have a prismatic quality, that an actor can use in such a way as to hint at wider meanings, things unsaid, lying behind them. Essentially, it's a highly organised simplicity.

Sunday 15   Read through the play. Some of it seems so utterly leaden it's difficult to see any evidence of six months' work. Not that six months is a long time on a project this size, but I'm conscious of the fact that I'm quite a slow writer and we are not working on an open schedule. Other points, though, I'm pleased with. Definite progress. The scene in which Tom and Casy meet for the first time has always worked well. And even though I've cut and re-written as dialogue some of Casy's monologues, Casy is still the narrational backbone and will still, I think, distance the audience slightly from the Joads. The scene in Act Two at Hooper's Ranch where Tom, out walking at night, is stopped by a guard, and later crawls beneath the wire to meet Casy on the other side, is nicely reminiscent of his going into the car wrecking-yard in Act One, the yard itself surrounded by wire. Both these wire scenes create images of Tom going into, then out of prison.

Later: have a sudden thought of these two Americans arriving in white coats, little bleepers attached to their breast pockets, asking us to wait outside while they mutter something about doing what they can. I remember the last time I discussed a play with a producer. It was at the BBC. I was under the distinct impression that he liked it, a *Radio Times* billing was even mentioned, I think. Possibly a feature article. It was only later that I realised this was an ideal, the script as it stood he hated.

Monday 16   Glasgow: to the Compass Theatre Company production of *King Lear* at the Theatre Royal. Stage history, this: Sir Anthony Quayle, at 73, not only playing Lear but relentlessly touring the country and performing six nights a week.

His Lear is very different from Anthony Hopkins' prowling, bear-like, gravel voiced king I saw last year at the National. Quayle's is elderly, eyes still bright, mind still playfully keen, an avuncular, sentimental but isolated figure, barely tolerated by Goneril and Regan, the new generation for whom the opportunity of power suddenly presents itself in Lear's division of the kingdom. On the heath, his intellect buckling, he becomes even older, more frail, stumbling. His reaching down inside himself to resurrect dignity, not as a king but as a human being, becomes an enormous effort of will and memory. It is an intriguing study of disintegration.

Now, Pa Joad is not, of course, King Lear. Far from it. But *Lear* is partly about a journey to the limits of human faculties, how first the mind crumbles, then the body; first the faith, then the will to carry on. So there are parallels . . .

Wednesday 18   Mid-afternoon. Deconstructing Rose of Sharon and Connie. Phone rings.

Duncan: 'Can you come to a script meeting?'

'This minute?'

'They've just arrived. Ready to start work.'

I gather up my stuff, head round to his flat. He and Janet are putting up Rob and Albert for the week they're going to be here. Duncan introducing, indicating chairs, percolating coffee, appearing absolutely at home. Which he is, of course – I mean absolutely at home in this situation, on which so much depends. Realise that I'm actually in a supremely sensitive state.

We hang about for a bit, talking about departures, flight times, arrivals, trans-Atlantic post. Then coffee and a lot of unpacking of scripts, pads, pens.

Duncan and I sit either end of the long sofa, me contriving to appear relaxed, purposeful. Albert almost lies in the armchair, Rob makes a precise right-angle on the floor, legs outstretched, back pinning a large cushion against the wall. They have brought us an American Penguin paperback copy of the novel, taller and fatter than the English Pan edition I've been using, so we'll be working to the American pagination from now on.

A terrific beginning with a speech by Albert about how, when they heard of the idea to adapt the novel, thought it was impossible, impression confirmed by re-reading it, but having read play, even early draft as this is, enormous achievement, thematic realisation extraordinarily impressive, very distinctive, absolutely right choices made, etc., etc.

Rob nods, eyes roving between Albert and us. Rob is slim, grey-haired, casual, neat, watchful, serious. A mediator, perhaps. Albert is smaller, compact, wiry, curling hair brushed back from a high forehead. Large jaw, large teeth. Leans his head back as he speaks, screwing up his eyes as tight as possible.

'In Act One, Scene One . . . '

After such a brilliant résumé of the script's qualities, it now transpires that Albert thinks that Act One is not quite as magnificent as he'd given the impression it was. We go through the first scene line by line, looking for possible cuts, suggesting alternatives, testing rhythms. By some deft psychological outmanoeuvring – probably not that at all, just sensitivity on my part thinking it was – Albert is by now managing the discussion, which ceases to be a discussion but a lecture. He holds the script now closer, now further from his eyes, pulling his glasses down from his hair, pushing them back up again, raising and lowering his eyebrows, flopping the script into his lap with a 'Well, what the hell do we do?' expression. Rob looks around cautiously.

So we stagger on, a rough hike through Act One.

A minor hiatus when Albert announces that the first line on a particular page doesn't logically follow from the last line on the preceding one. I read out the lines, unable to see any incoherence. It turns out that the vital bottom line is missing from both Rob and Albert's scripts, the photocopying machine we used not having printed it. Checking reveals this has happened quite often. Something to do with the positioning of the paper, probably. Spend half an hour dictating and writing in.

The main Act One problems are where to cut, and some of the transitions from scene to scene. Scene Two, the Casy–Tom meeting, ends at the moment with Tom's account of his imprisonment and his not having heard from his father, Tom senior, for four years:

Casy: 'I ain' seen ol' Tom in a bug's age. How is he?'

Tom: 'Come along. Pa'll be glad to see you. He always said you had too long a pecker for a preacher.'

The pecker line refers back to Casy's guilty admission that, as a preacher, he had often taken a girl out and 'laid with her' after 'gettin' 'em talking in tongues' at meetings. My point is, the line ends the scene on an uplift – Tom's memory of Pa, an image of Pa's homespun wit, etc.

It turns our attention to Pa himself, appearing now on stage with Ma as the scene cuts to Tom's homecoming.

Albert's contention is that the line is good, but not where it is now. It creates too much of a jostle of speech when what we actually want to do is get on and see the family's reaction to Tom's return. We cut Tom's existing response to Casy's laid-with-her speech and insert the pecker line there.

But somehow we wander off discussing, or rather Albert interviewing us on, specific details. The evening deteriorates into Albert dredging up passages of Steinbeck from memory and, going through the glasses-up, glasses-down routine, searching for them in his copy of the novel. As he flicks the pages I notice with increasing impatience swathes marked in yellow highlighter pen. Duncan and I do a lot of catching of each other's eyes. Whose play is this?

We're clearly off on the wrong foot. Duncan is irritated, I'm troubled that I haven't made the opportunity for myself to outline the ideas and processes of the adaptation. Especially as this script does not indicate the changes I want to make, and a lot of their time would be wasted deciding their response to what I already consider dead wood. On top of this, both Rob and Albert keep referring to the film, Albert reminding Rob how such and such was done, Rob doing a lot of nodding, neither agreeing nor disagreeing . . .

Now, both Duncan and I have agreed to avoid the film. I saw it once, a long time ago, can't remember where or much about it. But our seeing it now would have been no help at all.

Home. Feel subdued and aggrieved.

Thursday 19   Morning: true, the Americans are running the game. But to run the game is the American way. The only thing to do is to make sure we're in there with them. We are supposed to be collaborating, after all, working for the best possible text. And, to be fair, what Albert may be doing is going through the script initially as quickly as he can, with us, to get everything clear in his own mind and find out which sections we think need most work before concentrating, with us, on those sections. And why not have passages marked in the novel? I have passages marked in mine. We have to be challenged on the script. Each and every line of it. So why wasn't I so rational last night? No trust, that's why. It takes trust and time to turn a collaboration of two into a collaboration of four.

Late morning: ring Duncan. Agree to forget yellow highlighter, but clamp down on film–play comparisons, get on equal terms with America. He proposes a policy of taking note of all their suggestions for cuts, additions, changes, deliberating them between ourselves, reporting back. This seems to me laborious, a kind of complex square-dancing, but agree it might be necessary.

Script meeting: has Rob the mediator intervened somehow? I don't know. But the meeting lasted well into the night mostly in an atmosphere of conciliation and co-operation. Agreed on several cuts, firming the text as it stands, rather than developing it. Albert, or Rob, suggests that Scene Nine, One-Eye, should be cut entirely, saving time and an actor, and as it's a reprise of the earlier petrol-station attendant scene, there would be no dramatic loss to the play

I resist this reprise argument. Although Tom assaults the petrol attendant, he is only aggressive towards One-Eye. The idea is to show Tom's maturing under Casy's influence. He is goaded by the petrol attendant's complaining that only the 'beggin' people' stop at his tumbledown shack, all the high-spending limousine owners patronising the company stations in town. Tom reacts to the implication they're beggars, punches him in the chest, and shows no remorse for doing so. However, when One-Eye tries to beg a lift from Tom and Al, Tom is aggressive but is then angry with himself. He also shows a consolidating family responsibility by refusing Al's suggestion that they slope off and have a few beers with money he's saved. I also propounded my prison symbolism and, I think, touched on the possible significance of the wrecking-yard manager only having one eye. The thing is, I tend to think aloud and my thoughts become domino-like. The glass of wine that I was at that moment waving expressively possibly contributed very slightly to my eloquence. Well, loquacity.

But in the end, One-Eye goes. And if One-Eye goes, then the Act Two scene with Tom at the wire at Hooper's will have to go too. But we'll deal with that later.

On the subject of the petrol-station attendant, Rob and Albert gently point out that in the States they have gas, not petrol. That's what I thought, but . . . Embarrassed at making such an elementary mistake, I flip through the novel to discover that the American edition, sure enough, reads gas, but that the English text, which I have been using, has been altered to read petrol. Why? Who by? And what else has been changed?

The other major suggestion is that Rob and Albert believe Noah, the eldest, mostly silent brother, should be included in the play. His brooding presence is a calm contrast to Tom and Al, his introspection provides a focus for family care and, after Grampa, he is the second loss to the family, leaving – as he does – at Needles to live by the Colorado River. And as the family losses chip away at the fragility of Pa, they reinforce Ma's determination. And whoever plays Noah gives us an extra actor to use in Act Two. A possible Persky.

We get on to discussing stage design. I'm very much in favour of as bare a stage as possible, am prepared to fight for it. Rob agrees. I think. Rob tends to keep his options open, though his comments and suggestions on the text are concise, incisive, and extremely helpful. Albert suggests a backdrop of a map of the mid-western United States, the Joads' journey picked out on it. He makes a cogent case, but I think it might be too literal.

Later, Albert suggests – I think I've got this right, it's very late – a small model truck, a toy, as a sort of totem, placed on one side, downstage. I think this is ludicrous.

Out into the freezing night air. Albert has been extolling the efficiency of the earplugs he wears in order to sleep at night in New York, and which he's brought to Edinburgh with him. He has a problem sleeping. I wonder how many other phobias he has. Americans are so open, I expect I'll get to know before too long. Most are pretty understandable in New York, I guess.

Friday 20   Morning: meeting with Duncan in the tiny office he has at the Netherbow Theatre. In fact, it's the photocopying room, space enough for the machine and a small desk and chair. The model truck suggestion was a joke, apparently. So why did I take it seriously?

A halt in script discussions has been called until Sunday. Rob and Albert are to look at Act Two together, which they have not as yet studied as closely as Act One, and I'm leaving for London to see the English Shakespeare Company at the Old Vic. On reflection, I'm very pleased with the progress made so far. The play is becoming leaner, clearer, and there is an unspoken agreement that Studio is going to produce it. After that initial false start, something like a team spirit is beginning to evolve.

Saturday 21   London: to the Old Vic with Vivien
to see *Henry IV Parts One and Two*, and *Henry V*, Michael Pennington
playing Hal and Henry V. Directed by Michael Bogdanov, the three-
play marathon runs, with breaks, from 10.30 a.m. to 10.45 p.m. The
gruelling part of it is not staying with Shakespeare, or the same actors for
so long. On the contrary, audiences rather enjoy these communal tests
of endurance. They come, like us, with rolls to eat and flasks to drink
from at intervals. No, the weariness for me, coming about half-way
through, comes from being with the same director, being able to, or
believing that I'm going to be able to, anticipate directorial interpretations and solutions. There were enough contemporary parallels in the
Henry IVs to predict the Falkland themes of *Henry V*, with its combat-
jacketed, machine-gun-waving monarch urging his troops on standing
on the gun turret of a bogged-down tank.

Possibly it's wearisome too, because, unlike *Nicholas Nickleby* which,
admittedly, was slightly shorter at eight hours, I have a good knowledge
of the narrative. And although it would be possible to write a marathon
Grapes, the fact that its narrative and details are so well known, especially
to Americans, and a fair proportion of our audience at the Fringe will be
American, I expect, would probably work against anything much longer
than three hours. And impact is not dependent on length.

Sunday 22   Feeling none too brilliant after a
night in the Nightrider, the overnight train on which you sit up for the
eight limb-crabbing hours it takes from King's Cross to Edinburgh.
Alternately sat up and lay folded into a *z* across the seat. It has the
advantage of being cheap (£19), but the advantage wears off by Finsbury
Park. I'm getting too old for this sort of thing. Vivien's coming back later
today.

Breakfast with Duncan, Janet, Rob, and Albert, who describes the last
time he and the Studio Productions company travelled from the midlands to Edinburgh by overnight bus. They crossed the Cheviots at
dawn. Hills as far as the horizon, over which the light was breaking. He
heard sheep bells (sheep bells?). It was 'real Brigadoon time', he says,
taking the last croissant, 'real Brigadoon time'.

Look through Act One. I want to start the play with the lights coming
up on the whole cast, then slowly fading down to a solitary tenant: 'Ever'
year we got a good crop comin'. Then the wind come . . .' Decide to
re-work this, so that now the lights fade down to pick out Tom Joad,

speaking a short, amended passage from Chapter 6: 'Night after night in my bunk I figgered how she'd be when I come home again . . . But I know'd it wouldn't be the same as it was'. The lights fade out, Tom disappears, lights fade up on the rest of Scene One – the tenant, owner, tenant and tractor man, used-car salesman. We next see Tom in the following Tom–Casy scene. This, for me, makes that whole beginning to the play, over which I had so many problems, fall into place.

Several cuts and adjustments made, views questioned, defended. We argue, when we argue, with the decorum of discussing. It has taken me four days to feel that I'm on equal terms with the Americans, and that the concepts behind the writing have been fully explained. Perhaps as a result of this, and of seeing *The Henrys*, the actors sweeping quickly on and off an almost bare stage, the performance fast and fluid, I'm much more confident in being freer with the characters in *Grapes*. Cutting away anything that slows things up, getting a real momentum going. The time of careful research and wallcharting is perhaps over.

Duncan, meanwhile, has been putting most of Act One on to a word processor.

One major change: the name Studio Theatre Productions is no more. When this came about, I don't know, but the company is now to be known as American Festival Theatre.

Monday 23   Act Two: the more difficult of the two acts. Rob and Albert delighted with Persky and Bird. Agree to cut some of the more purple phrasing from Persky's speech to the Bakersfield Association.

One note similar to the petrol–gas: nobody in California, says Albert, owns or works on a farm – they have ranches.

The main problem with the Act is the lead-up to the Weedpatch dance and the dance sequence itself. We are all agreed we should avoid portraying the dance on stage, but since the Persky–Bird–Adams scene was cut, all the exposition of the intended raid is reported by Tom, a long and unwieldy speech with which nobody is happy.

'Dramatise, dramatise,' says Albert.

If a Mr Thomas–Wallace–Tom scene is written, Rob assures me there will be no problem casting it. I now have very little idea of the size of cast the play demands, but the Americans are confident the play will have the actors it needs. It's a very different attitude from that confronting Fringe plays produced in this country or, for that matter, any play produced anywhere in Britain, where as small a cast as possible is crucial. I shouldn't imagine a straight play running in London at the moment outside the subsidised National or Royal Shakespeare Company, has a cast in double figures, even.

Looking at the Weedpatch section, Scenes Two (at the camp), Three (preparing for the dance), and Four (Tom–Al–Higgins), I propose re-writing Scene Two, alternating Ma, Pa, and Rose of Sharon (the camp facilities, Rose's bewilderment at Connie's leaving), with Thomas, Wallace, and Tom (Thomas being forced to reduce their wages); reverting to Ma and Pa (the camp management committees, etc.), and then back to Thomas, Wallace, and Tom (the dance raid tip-off). Scene Three, Tom's reporting, to be cut, and a new passage, Pa asking how the Camp Entertainment Committee intends to prevent the fight, written in. Scene Four, with necessary adjustments, then follows as is.

This will, hopefully, give the sequence a flow and an edge. And it has the advantage of including information previously lost – that Thomas tips off Tom and Wallace not only because he is sympathetic to the migrants but also because the Farmers Association pressured him to drop his wages, and that Pa is no longer suspicious of the camp managers' motives but reliant on their decisions. For Scene Four, I reassert that as the One-Eye scene has been lost, it is important that although Tom is aggressive in his questioning of Higgins, he uses no physical violence and restrains Al from doing so.

Rob suggests using the old woman from a previous Weedpatch chapter, Chapter 22, who torments Rose of Sharon that 'clutch and hug dancing' resulted in another girl's baby being born dead. 'Spooky lady', as Rob calls her, would provide substance to Rose of Sharon's hysteria, and at the moment we lose sight of her somewhat in this sequence.

I'm not at all sure of this, as I think it is out of context with the conventions of the play. Rob agrees, but believes that is precisely why it might achieve a dramatic resonance as something happening almost within Rose of Sharon's mind.

I agree to try it and see.

Tuesday 24   Meet Hal Easton, American Festival Theatre's executive producer, for the first time. He, Rob, and Albert, Duncan and I meet in Duncan's miniscule office, where Hal reports that he has officially secured the Netherbow Theatre for *The Grapes of Wrath*. We open on the first day of the Festival, 10 August,

47

running daily except Sundays until the end, 29 August. Rob will direct the play, and hold auditions for actors in New York and Chicago. The cast will arrive in Edinburgh to start rehearsals at the beginning of July.

The other plays in AFT's repertoire will be staged at the Royal Scots Club, a large regimental club in the New Town, a couple of hundred yards or so from the Assembly Rooms. Hal will have an office there and a vast basement room converted into a theatre, which AFT will also sub-let to other American companies, the entire operation being under Hal's control. The full AFT acting company will number about forty, most actors appearing in more than one show. *Grapes*, though, is being given priority.

Hal is tall, slim, with thinning hair, a goatee beard, intensively bright eyes. He quivers with energy and talks fast, firing off statements like pistol shots. According to Duncan, he used to be a child TV star. Rob and Albert, jammed against the door, peer over his shoulder; I perch on the desk behind Duncan. He and Hal stand shoulder to shoulder between us, negotiating paperwork. I am quite happy to leave this side of things to Duncan. He is a businessman, an orchestrator, urbane, relaxed, but with a needle-sharp sense of fairness. Not that AFT have been anything other than scrupulously straightforward, generous in fact, in their dealings with us so far. But Duncan's is the business voice in our partnership. It's as simple as that.

Later, script – Act Two. The wire scene at Hooper's is cut. Tom's narration of the family moving from Hooper's to the boxcars is re-distributed among himself, Ma, and Pa and, to Albert's 'Dramatise, dramatise', dramatised.

A long discussion on Al's bride-to-be, Aggie Wainwright, who appears neither in the play nor the novel, although her parents do. They live (and presumably so does Aggie), in the other half of the Joad boxcar. Mrs Wainwright helps Ma at the delivery of Rose of Sharon's baby, while Mr Wainwright helps Pa, Al, and others build the bank to try to stop the river flooding too far.

Both Rob and Albert contend that Aggie should appear in the play and the parents should be cut. I agree. But where to write her in? Do we want to be introduced to another crucial character only ten minutes off the end of the play? At the moment, Al reports his intention to get married. Isn't this enough?

I am reluctant to destroy the dramatic build to the climax of the play, the rain, Rose of Sharon's confession to Ma of her betrayal of Tom, Ma and Tom's last meeting in the culvert where he is hiding, cutting immediately to the flood–stillbirth and then the final scene in the barn, by working in an Al and Aggie love story. And just sketching it in is not going to be sufficient. Such a small detail would be overwhelmed by everything else that's going on.

Although the whole ending of the play, from the boxcars on, is going to be re-written, I see it almost as the final movement of a symphony, where all the major themes are resolved. And I think all these are within Tom, Ma, and Rose of Sharon. By now, Pa and Al are minor ones, played out.

Albert suggests that Al meets Aggie at the Weedpatch dance. But then why does she and her family go to the boxcars? Just because she is in love with Al? Why didn't he stay behind with her?

Search through the script for other possible places to introduce Aggie. None stand out as obvious. It'll have to be near the end, I think. An advantage of Aggie is that she can help Ma with Rose of Sharon, and so be there when Al says they're getting married. And I might be able to work something with Al – show a character development from girl-chasing lad to mature adult.

Another point is that Al and Aggie are in many ways the new Connie and Rose of Sharon. But they're realists. Their marriage will work out. And I like the idea of showing the growth of their relationship somehow.

But the ending is a huge challenge. Dangerous, exciting. I can't allow the structure to collapse. These final scenes could so easily become melodramatic, sentimental. In fact, I could open the play up to the very same critical accusations levelled at Steinbeck. I can't allow it to become lush when it has to be raw.

Wednesday 25   Another long, and this time finally acrimonious, discussion on the ending of the play. It emerges that Rob has a similar idea to my own, that Tom remains on stage until the close. The culvert scene he has with Ma is played, almost in darkness, at the side or the rear of the stage; the plan is that he remains there alone as a shadowy 'witness' to the similarly low-lit stillbirth–flood and barn sequence. At the end a light fades up on Rose of Sharon, wrapped in a blanket, nursing the dying man. A second low light fades up on Tom, ten or so feet away. So brother and sister share the final stage image, apart but united. And as Tom begins the play, so he now ends it. We take his 'I'll be all around in the dark. I'll be everywhere . . . Why, I'll be there', speech out of the culvert scene and use it as the final lines of the play. Or rather, leave an indication of it in the culvert scene (he tells Ma he plans to do 'what Casy done' but 'I ain't thought it out clear yet'), but the meat of it goes at the end, the intervening sequence acting as a kind of bridge. Once over that bridge, he knows exactly what he's going to do. He has accepted Casy, understood Casy, become his successor. It is as if he understands, finally, by 'seeing' Rose of Sharon give life to the starving, as if 'knowing' that his mother and sister will survive, Tom's spirit is set brilliantly, soaringly free. Now he, too, will go on.

It is exactly the ending the play needs. I feel enormously fired by it. Duncan, though, calls a halt. He is seriously perturbed at the idea and leads me into another room for a private conference, muttering about our having a policy of considering major changes between ourselves before working them through with the Americans. Door closed, he accuses me of contravening our agreement. Actually, I have, but I retaliate by saying that a play can't be written by two sides giving each other formal notices, that ideas, particularly good ones (I suppose I mean mine, or those that I like), should be explored between the four of us. He is adamant that the idea is not a good one, that Tom leaves the stage at the culvert scene, as he does in the novel. I say he's being far too literal, seeing the play not as a play but as a book.

He challenges, I explain the idea. Again. Again. It's very late, we're both tired and the atmosphere between us begins almost to crackle electrically. I'm simmering (hopefully camouflaging it, though possibly not), and I suspect his temper is not at a perfect equilibrium either. There are other currents here, too, besides the purely artistic question of how to finish the play. In fact, it's a psychological junction box. He feels that I have broken our 'policy' and perhaps wilfully distorting *The Grapes*, while I feel passionately that he asked me to write this play and that while his ideas, opinions, and advice are crucial, I must be free to explore the direction I feel is right.

But eventually he concedes. We'll try the ending. The encounter leaves me shaken, but a mutual trust and respect has evolved since September and, I suppose, has just passed its first test.

Thursday 26   Hal, Rob, and Albert leave for New York. They take with them a word processor print-out of Act One of the revised draft of *Grapes One* – what will become, when complete, *Grapes Two*. Everyone in good spirits. There is a feeling of confidence about the project.

This morning and afternoon at the BBC to record my presentation for the radio documentary on Graham Vick that Vivien Devlin is producing, cueing in my script with the music and the interviews with Graham Vick, Janice Cairns, Sir Peter Hall, and others. One of the music inserts is the very beginning of *Don Giovanni*: a long note, a long pause, a second long note. The engineer suggests shortening the pause. 'Much more dramatic,' he says. He's right.

APRIL

Thursday 2 During the past few days, I have been working on re-writes and discussing them with Duncan. And I've found that I've changed, nothing that radical, details really, but still changed, some of the script decisions we made when Rob and Albert were here. But I'm obsessive with words. I know this. Still not happy with the dance sequence, which I've started over and over again without getting very far, let alone actually finishing, probably in the belief that if I keep bashing away at the run-up and get that right at least, the momentum will propel me into such a magnificent long jump the sequence will somehow write itself. It hasn't. Finally end up with an inelegant plough into the sand. Duncan doesn't raise any objections though, but that's hardly the point.

Nightly, Duncan and I have closeted ourselves in his office, buttoning *Grapes Two* into the word processor. Up until now I have used my typewriter ('Still using one of those? And paper, too?' said Rob), and I miss the feeding in of the paper, the thack-thack of its keys, the resulting pile of printed pages, its reassurance. The luminous plasticity, the comparative silence, the remoteness of word processing harasses me. Each night we switch the machine on, shove the disc into the slot, the cursor chokes across the screen leaving a green tail of dotted, square-shaped letters, words subliminally pulsing, pulling the retina, inducing violent eye-strain, headaches, and God knows what else.

More than this. The machine needs to be mollycoddled. To get it to print, to get out what you've put in, its printer, a plastic tray with a roller lying across it, has to be positioned just so beside the machine, the concertinaed paper just so beside it, rolled through and squared-up just so, or else it will refuse to print. A millimetre, a touch, is the difference between smooth operation or total refusal. When it does print, its metal beak jabbing, it has to be watched constantly. Sometimes, arbitrarily, it stops, humming its almost inaudible defiant hum, defiant because it's inaudible, then, just as suddenly, its mean little cackle starts up again. Blasted thing.

But finally we have a square, half-inch thick *Grapes Two*, floppy in your hands like a fish, impossible to read without it sliding all over the floor. And neither is it shorter than *Grapes One*. Although Act One falls to 57 pages, Act Two increases to 74, a total of 131 – 6 pages longer. Cutting One-Eye and Hooper's wire has reduced Act One to eleven scenes, Act Two to fourteen.

We send the completed draft to Rob. The plan is to re-write and liaise with them by trans-Atlantic post and the odd phone call, aiming to have *Grapes Three*, the rehearsal draft, ready by the end of May.

Friday 3   Glasgow: to the RSC's *Kiss Me Kate*, directed by Adrian Noble, with Paul Jones and Nichola McAuliffe. Fast, glitzy and enjoy it enormously, in the same way as you enjoy lemon meringue pie. It's not particularly filling but very good once in a while.

Thursday 9   Glasgow: to interview Spanish actress and director Nuria Espert, directing an opera for the first time, *Madam Butterfly* for Scottish Opera.

She is a great actress and a formidable woman. For years in the vanguard of opposition to censorship and the oppressive shadow of Franco, she was the first to stage Sartre and Brecht in Spain, but only succeeded in producing Lorca's *Yerma* there after a triumphant performance in the title role at the 1972 London World Theatre Season. She played Dona Rosita at the 1983 Edinburgh Festival and revived *Yerma* at Edinburgh in 1986. She directed an English company led by Glenda Jackson and Joan Plowright, in Lorca's *The House of Bernarda Alba*, in London last year.

Nuria Espert is small; a handsome, angular face with deep-set almost ebony eyes, a wide, expressive mouth, very white, square teeth. She buries her fingers in her long jet hair as she speaks, draws them out, making fluttering movements as she circles her hands in the air. Acting, she says, isn't about all this – she tosses her head back, claps a hand over her heart – sometimes it is not about movement at all. It is about stillness, and – she touches her temples, widens her eyes – the text, its real, inner meaning, working through the mind. Sometimes it is enough just to be perfectly still. With absolute control and concentration.

Certainly *Bernarda Alba* was tense with control. Lorca's plays are not journeys, they're studies, casebooks of time and place. All his work whirls centrifugally around the theme of emotional frustration, a life-draining search for love and spiritual freedom. Like Beckett, it is the depth, not the breadth of vision that makes Lorca so powerful a dramatist, the depth of imaginative truth.

Monday 13 Sign the contract Duncan has negotiated on our behalf with AFT, which is basically their undertaking to produce the play at the Festival, and that nothing in the script can be altered by either party without mutual consultation. Later Duncan will organise their performance licence.

We also mail a copy of *Grapes Two* to Adline Finlay at English Theatre Guild, now re-naming themselves Chappell Plays. Must be the year for name changes.

The Graham Vick programme broadcast tonight. Listened to make sure the tape had got safely from Edinburgh to the BBC Centre at Glasgow. Never trust anyone.

Friday 24 Adline Finlay sends us a copy of a contract from lawyers representing Elaine Steinbeck, John Steinbeck's widow, to be signed by both her and us. It comprises two closely-typed pages which, boiled down, means that as Mrs Steinbeck now holds the copyright of the novel (copyright was renewed by John Steinbeck in 1967, the year before he died), she also retains a play using the title and the characters, etc., etc.

It's as much as I expected. But presumably this means the script has the approval of the Estate. I wonder who, exactly, approved it? Does it mean that Elaine Steinbeck has actually read it?

I find it difficult to imagine either of the Steinbecks. I don't think I've ever seen a picture of John Steinbeck, although I feel I've almost come to know him personally, or at least his big, broad-chested ghost that perhaps looks over my shoulder at what I'm writing every now and then, sometimes carping, sometimes without too much indignation. Hopefully he'd still claim progenitorship of whatever eventually reaches the stage.

Mrs Steinbeck, I know nothing about. I would like to meet her.

News from AFT: first cast change. They want a Granma instead of a Grampa. They're having difficulty finding a good, elderly actor but have a good, and presumably elderly, actress in mind who would also double as the Old Woman in the dance sequence.

Saturday 25 Thinking over the Granma proposal, a Granma might well be better for the play than a Grampa, emphasising the biological chain of life, and the matriarchal strength of the women. Grampa doesn't actually stand for anything in the play, other than a strand of garrulous humour. Although Granma is Pa's mother (I don't think we need change it so she becomes Ma's instead), her substitution for Grampa would add a vital and discreet thematic link.

Duncan takes professional advice on the Steinbeck contract. I take my copy for two friends to see: Alma Cullen, a playwright, and her husband, James Cullen. They are, as always, very supportive, and generous with their time and advice. At this stage in the game, talking the project over with Alma, who is clear-sighted and sagacious in anything to do with writing and bubblingly optimistic in her outlook on life, is both beneficial and calming.

An acquaintance of Alma's has just had an American disaster. A play of his which did reasonably well in London and transferred to Broadway with a big American star in the lead closed after four nights, after an almighty battering from the critics. 'Who'd be in showbusiness?' says Alma.

Who, indeed? All this and we might not even get an audience. Who knows?

A thought which a feature article in tonight's *Evening News* does nothing to allay. Hal has been busy, having engineered an interview for himself, Rob, and Albert when they were over here in March. Apart from the fact that it's not at all well written (not surprising for the *Evening News*), what good it does three months ahead of the Festival, I haven't a clue. There's some waffle attributed to Albert that his job as literary manager means he represents the author, looking after his interests, though which author this refers to isn't made clear. Rob: 'It will be a very theatrical adaptation by necessity . . . how do you have half the United States on stage?' The short answer is, you don't try. Not on a stage measuring twenty feet by twenty.

The cast, apparently, will be about a dozen. Nice to know.

Wednesday 29   A signed Steinbeck contract goes back to Adline Finlay.

Word filters through about Steppenwolf, of whom we have not heard for some time. They have long held an option on the novel, but their stage adaptation has never been completed. Now, apparently, their wheels are in motion. I bet they are. Who is writing it, and what structure it's taking, I don't know (do I want to?), but it seems to be well underway.

The understanding is they will open in Chicago, hope to transfer to New York and, if possible, London.

Whatever happens, it doesn't alter the fact that ours is the first to be authorised, and will be the first to have its world première. And at the Edinburgh Festival. It's not exactly David and Goliath – yet – but it does give me a spur to develop the play further, a determination to scale that mountain before a more widely-known and financially better-equipped team. What we need is not only to get to the peak but also to have the best possible flag to plant once we're there. And then we need a good Edinburgh. Good production, performances, audiences, reviews. Suddenly you realise just how many more rockfaces there are to cling on to and climb, how many more ravines to cross, just how far off the summit we are.

As to the script, I've written in Noah, the stoic, brooding presence, and rewritten Rose of Sharon. I'm now much more sure of where she's going – Act Two is her Act in many ways. Connie Rivers needs more definition. In my pages of character notes, the entry under his name has the most question marks. In the novel, of course, Connie and Rose of Sharon are living with his family. Well, I haven't alluded to that, not wanting to get bogged down in the problem of if his family is going to California too, as would seem likely, why he and Rose of Sharon don't go with them. I'm allowing the audience to assume they are travelling with the Joads so that Ma can help her daughter with the baby. But what exactly is Connie? A dreamer, certainly. All these castles he builds in the air: taking a correspondence course, owning a store, getting a house with an ice-maker. Is he a weakling? I don't think so. It's not as simple as that. He's 'of a Texan strain', the Joads travel through Texas, yet Connie doesn't leave her to go back to the old places. More of a Don Juan, maybe. And when does he make up his mind to leave his pregnant wife? In the heat of the moment during the chaos at Hooverville? Or was it all pre-planned and he's waiting for a suitable opportunity? If so, when did he make the decision? If it was before they drive across the Mojave Desert, then it makes his love-making to Rose of Sharon up on the back of the truck at night a particularly cruel act.

And why does he leave her? Does he know that Rose of Sharon will sooner or later see the pictures he so lavishly paints of the life ahead of them as the fakes they are, and believe that she will then reject him? Or is it that he can't, when it comes down to it, face the reality of getting any job he can and help bring up baby?

And when he does leave, where does he go? To Persky's peach ranch?

56

Eventually decide that he's a bit of a Don Juan, but genuinely in love with Rose of Sharon, and he doesn't leave her without some guilt. The power of her love, which is almost cloying, destabilises the buccaneering image he has of himself.

I write in more lines for them in the early scenes, building their relationship, but leave several questions unanswered. Their few lines in the last scene of Act One, the prelude to their making love, the last time we see them together, in fact, are a problem. They always have been. It used to be because they were difficult to write, and I still think it will be difficult to make them work well on stage – but that's as much an actor's and director's problem as a writer's. The real problem now is that I have to decide whether that scene between them should reaffirm their love or become the symbol of its dereliction. Our perceptions of Connie come home to roost in that scene, and I can't decide which way to take it until I know when he decides to leave her.

I don't think the process of Connie's disaffection should necessarily be apparent to the audience except in retrospect, but it's important that I know. And the actor, of course. At the moment, the love-making prelude is as it is in the book. A cuddly get-together.

Another point: the Joads are indigenous Oklahomans, Connie is not. Perhaps there is an underlying, unsaid friction between them, exacerbated somewhat when Tom returns. What is Tom's reaction to Connie and how does Connie respond? In the novel, Tom has met Connie before his imprisonment, but does not know him well. In the play, I think they meet for the first time at Tom's homecoming. And while Tom has been away, Connie has assumed Tom's position as Pa's deputy in the family hierarchy. (That place would normally go to the eldest son, but Noah cannot assume the responsibility. Al is younger than Tom or Connie.) But now Tom is back, the family regroup and Connie is edged sideways. Tom perhaps sees him as an interloper. At any rate, he'd be watchful of any man who married his sister. Connie possibly resents all this. Rose of Sharon notices it. And a perceptible strain between Connie and Tom in the early scenes would stoke Rose of Sharon's later antagonism towards her brother.

Thursday 30   Re-writes. I had thought I'd left wallcharts and structure diagrams behind, but I'm back to them. It almost seems sometimes that successive revisions, instead of rendering the play more spare and coherent, cause it to fall apart in my hands. Far from being resolved, problems are multiplying. But whereas before all my mapping out was of the book, the expeditions I'm making now are entirely of the play. I've left the book behind. Haven't looked at it for some time. The play and I are at last creating our own landscape. Progress.

MAY

Monday 4   London: National Theatre – *Antony and Cleopatra*, directed by Peter Hall at the Olivier, with Anthony Hopkins and Judi Dench. A vast, majestic, enthralling experience, cinematic in its pace and panoramic sweep, cutting from public roisterings to private conferences, from passion to politics, in a second. Acted with dazzling verve and confidence. A production suffused in deep plum colours, the reds of rich velvets and dried blood. Apart from two great double doors set in a partial and movable semi-circle of crumbling wall, an open stage. *Antony and Cleopatra* is a middle-aged love affair with the foolhardiness of youth, played out under the scrutiny of friends and servants, an infatuation leading the world into chaos.

An extraordinary delivery of Enobarbus' Act II barge speech by Michael Bryant. Enobarbus, a working soldier, northern accent, a chap who's been about a bit, seen a lot, takes the chair only just vacated by Caesar, hooks one leg over one of its arms, and gives the speech as reminiscence, slowly and quietly describing everything as carefully and as impressively as he can, knowing he's got a good story and, in Agrippa and Maecenas, a captive audience.

How effective restraint is. In this case the product of meticulous analysis of the text, the actor and director knowing exactly what they're doing.

Thursday 7   London: National Theatre – an icy production of Ibsen's *Rosmersholm* at the Cottesloe. Not surprising to find this was Freud's favourite play. The text, yeasty with sexual and emotional repression and guilt, the characters' past being peeled away as the play moves forward, must have caught the contemporary fascination for, and fear of, psychoanalysis. The play itself is very much a prototype for *Hedda Gabler*: for Rebekka read Hedda; Rosmer, Tesman; Kroll, Judge Brack; Mortensgaard, Lovborg.

Freud made this kind of play, repression as drama, impossible to write again. A reason why Ibsen is absolutely locked into his own time, why he represents the late nineteenth century, why an updated production would never work. But Ibsen must be hugely technically demanding for actors. Lose that tightrope tension once, lose that total attention from the audience and you lose the play, it'd sag and flop into irretrievable melodrama.

59

But I do find Ibsen heavy going. Even in as clear a translation as this (by Frank McGuinness), and with a Rebekka as flinty and as fiercely, finely controlled as Suzanne Bertish's.

Saturday 9   London: burrowing around a second-hand bookshop in Charing Cross Road, come across a small pile of volumes of the Steinbeck letters, co-edited by Elaine Steinbeck. The frontispiece, of course, a black-and-white photograph of J.S. Oval face, clipped black moustache and beard, dark eyes wary, mouth set in a guarded, almost sceptical expression, as if impatient for the camera. Perhaps he didn't like having his picture taken much. It's rather unnerving that I'd entirely forgotten about this photograph. My mental image of him is older, more bear-like.

National Theatre: *Yerma* at the Cottesloe, Juliet Stevenson memorable in the title role. The audience sit on opposite sides of a square of paving, central stairs dividing them into four blocks. The stairs used very creatively as the Andalusian landscape, the actors criss-crossing them as they go up or down as if walking over uneven, tufted ground, as if used to carrying heavy bundles of washing, agricultural implements. A sense of the outdoors, the heat; a lot of wrists rubbing foreheads, sweat wiped out of eyes and from the backs of necks. We should watch for this in *The Grapes*. The dust, the heat, the sense of people used to the earth, the great landscape.

Monday 11   A letter from New York, enclosing Albert's suggested re-writes for Granma. What he's done is merely transfer Grampa's lines (and, therefore, character) to Granma, throwing in a garnish of a 'Pu-raise God for vittory!' here, and a 'Full o' grace an' glory!' there.

All this religious whooping it up by Granma is there in the novel all right, but it irritates me and I'm sure it would never work on stage. It's what Duncan calls the hillbilly part of the book. Besides, I've taken great care to play down the overt religious themes in favour of others I find more interesting and which I think will work better dramatically. Disconcerted that apparently Albert hasn't seen this. Or perhaps he thinks I've just missed the religious element and is trying to reinstate it. Whichever way, we're not connecting on one of the basic strands of the play. But I'm disconcerted even more by the fact that he seems to believe one character's lines can simply be foisted onto another.

I'm just going ahead and completing my own characterisation. Type it all up and add a soothing letter.

What I want to do is use Granma to underline the idea of the family as a biological and historical process. I've cut Grampa's (Granma's if Albert has his way) comic entrance from Tom's homecoming scene. Ma now says that Grampa died some time ago, since when Granma has sat mostly by herself. The audience should assume she's in a state of shock, reclusive.

Granma first appears at the family huddle, when they're deciding when to leave home. When Tom suggests that Jim Casy comes with them, I've written in a line for Connie that 'he ain' family'. Suddenly Granma breaks her silence: 'You ain' been family too long, Connie Rivers'. Therefore she is the first to confront Connie. Perhaps she distrusts him.

The next day, the family preparing to leave, Granma (as Grampa did) refuses to go. Her reasons, though, are different, and I've taken some of the impetus here from Muley Graves, the character in an earlier part of the book who stays behind 'like an ol' graveyard ghos' ' when his family sets off west. Granma says she was born on this land, bore Pa here, believes that Rose of Sharon should bear her child here. She talks about how it is wrong to 'tear your roots outa your own land', referring to both family history and their cropping livelihood; she rounds on Ma, telling her 'it ain't natural', soliciting Ma's complicity as a woman and foreshadowing, perhaps, Rose of Sharon's own tragic labour. She accuses Pa of breaking family tradition: 'You ask that preacher', the preacher being the guide in all things. The irony is that there is no way she can stay behind (they drug her with soothing syrup mixed in coffee to get her onto the truck, as they did previously with Grampa), and that Casy no longer sees himself as a preacher.

The death scene I've re-written to focus more clearly on the women and imply a sense of Granma handing the matriarchal baton on to Ma. Her death is both a premonition and an accusation.

Friday 15   A six-page letter from Rob. He has cast the play and has an ensemble of nine men and five women. Albert himself will play Pa Joad. Don't know what to make of this at all. Both Duncan and I knew that Albert is an actor, but neither of us can see him as Pa.

Their being in New York and our being in Edinburgh doesn't help. As neither of us have been along to any of the auditions, we're relying solely on Rob's judgement. Albert may have auditioned along with other prospective Pa Joads and given the best reading. Or he might not – it's persuasive from this distance to suspect a bit of insider dealing. And as Albert is a staff member of the production company, there's little that Duncan and I can easily say at this stage. Any subsequent stage, of course, will be too late.

Just as worrying are the problems that could arise with having a dramaturg also a leading actor. The situation's alive with ghastly possibilities. Duncan and I might be surreptitiously pushed out of things. Well, I won't be pushed. Neither will Duncan. It's a potentially enormous political and personal strain that would destroy rehearsals, and I'm determined not to have the play endangered by anything like that. Albert will have to leave dramaturgy outside the rehearsal room door, that's all.

There is a problem over the casting of the Barn Boy, the son of the dying man at the end, who has four lines and will be changed to Barn Girl and played by the actress playing Aggie Wainwright unless we can find a young actor here good enough to be coached in the accent by Rob.

This is something I'd half foreseen. But the actress playing Aggie will probably be in her early twenties, Aggie herself being about seventeen. The Barn Boy is, I should imagine, about nine, at a stretch, twelve. A young-looking twenty can age down to seventeen, but never twelve. On the other hand, it would be equally disastrous to have a nine-year-old local boy march on three minutes off the end of the show, open his mouth, and a badly obscured Scots accent lurch out. Unreconstructed Scots accents are insidiously pervasive. Perhaps someone at the American Consulate has a young son. Or the American school might be able to help.

The casting of the Tom–Wallace–Thomas sequences is in question as well. Because none of the actors playing the Joads (with the exception of Noah), Connie, or Casy will double, and those that are will have either just done so or be about to, there is nobody immediately available to play Mr Thomas without creating confusion for the audience.

Rob suggests that Thomas changes sex, that we have a Mrs Thomas instead, to be played by the same actress who plays Sairy Wilson in Act One. There were, he says, many female ranchers in California.

This sets alarm bells ringing. The play will have the cast it needs, they said. Well, I don't mind a Granma instead of a Grampa, in fact it's much better, I'm prepared to do everything I can to find a preferably American Barn Boy, but Thomas was a part I wrote at their instigation on the understanding the play needed it and after being assured the casting was no problem. Now it turns out that a problem is exactly what it is. I suspect it's mainly my intense frustration at not being able to discuss this with Rob personally and immediately, that makes me (and Duncan) doubt his word about female ranchers, but at the same time, I don't think a female Thomas is dramatically viable.

A similar problem over Higgins, the man whom Tom and Al man-handle from the dance where he has tried to pick a fight. Who is to play Higgins? Somewhere between Edinburgh and New York this section of the play is becoming confused, one of the problems of working primarily by post, where every reference has to be meticulously annotated and dated, every question polished to glass-like clarity so there's no dubiety anywhere.

Duncan sees through the fog almost immediately, pointing out that it is of secondary importance which of the doubling actors plays Higgins, as he is not the focus of the scene, Tom and Al are. It is not a casting but a staging problem. If it is played in less than half light (it is outside at night), with Higgins facing upstage and Tom and Al downstage, Higgins can easily be played by the actor playing Floyd at the top of the Act. Such a simple solution, I wonder why Rob never thought of it. Or me.

So Higgins is no great concern, but the Thomas news is disturbing. I hope all those assurances in March weren't made without thought of the practicalities and budget involved. That way compromises and disasters lie.

Apart from this, a good suggestion for a cut in Act One, plus a question on the ending of the Tom meeting Casy scene. The ending which Rob and Albert fought for in March: Tom: 'Come along. Pa'll be glad to see you,' Rob now says is 'too yellow brick road'. He proposes putting back the 'too long a pecker for a preacher' line (!) or using the chicken story from Chapter 6, which Tom tells to Casy and Muley Graves, about Ma, about to cut the head off a chicken with an axe, chasing a too persistent tin peddler and, forgetting which hand was holding what, beating him with a live chicken. I like it. Decide to give it to Casy to tell Tom as Ma appears at the rear of the stage for the homecoming scene.

Act Two suggestions are mostly the elimination of a couple of simple errors, someone saying 'tonight' when it is in fact already night, and for cuts, most of which deal with the same theme, Pa's loss of authority within the family. This, I agree, is over-written in the script as it stands, and I go along with several of Rob's ideas, taking out a lot of surplus, especially from the stillbirth–flood section. Even though I guarded against over-writing from the word go, or thought I did, there is still much that can come out. Cut, cut, is the technique of writing. A litter of words help nobody. As long as the line of Pa's defeat is clearly there in the text, that is all an actor needs to give a vivid account of it. All Albert needs to give a vivid account . . . Worries, worries . . .

Some suggestions I turn down. Such as the cutting of a few lines from the sequence at Weedpatch where Ma accuses the family of avoiding the reality of their having no work and the money almost having run out. However much they like Weedpatch after Hooverville, they will have to move on. Pa reacts – why is a woman making all the decisions now? Ma – 'You get some bacon inside this family before you say what's good for them.' This is the gist of it, but I want to retain their confrontation in full. It's not very long, but it is important in defining Ma and Pa's relationship, especially after the Act One jack-handle episode, the first time Ma openly defied one of Pa's pronouncements. This is not a reprise of that scene. Here, she is conceding that Pa has the right as head of the family to plan on their behalf, but only when he is fulfilling his side of the contract by being the provider. Yet, as she explains to Tom after Pa walks out in anger, her rebellion was merely a strategy. What Ma and Pa are actually doing is calling up the grit in each other; she is reaffirming the love and respect she has for him. So Tom understands a little more about family politics, which he might later put into practice.

I have done quite a bit of carpentry on the night-time culvert scene independently of Rob or Albert. It now ends with an indication of the 'I'll be there' speech, so building the first part of the bridge, the other end of which ends the play:

Tom: 'I'll be all around in the dark. I'll be ever'where – wherever you look. An' then . . . See? I'm talkin' like Casy already. Sometimes it seems like I can even see him.'

Ma: 'It's like I' blin' it's so dark. Let me touch you . . . I wanna remember even if it's only my fingers rememberin' . . . '

I'm rather pleased with this scene in the rain, ending with Ma touching Tom's scarred face and cutting immediately to the screams of Rose of Sharon in labour and the crash of renewed storm. Also, it juxtaposes speeches two pages apart in the book to give a nice word play on the image of sight – Tom: '*seems* like I can even *see* . . . '; Ma: 'It's *like* I' *blin*' . . . '

No responses in Rob's letter about the lines I've written into *Grapes Two* for Al and Aggie, one section inserted between the first, general scene in the boxcar, and the scene where Rose of Sharon confesses to Ma she has betrayed Tom. Two people discussing marriage plans. It's very short, very uninspired and very uninspiring. Perhaps Rob diplomatically thought it best not to comment, assuming that I will of course be re-writing. For which I'm grateful. And I will be re-writing.

Rob's major point is one we discussed briefly in March, that the play needs much more of the wry humour and earthiness of the novel to give it a buoyancy and something for the drama to work against. What we are arriving at is a lean, raw play, but one that is almost entirely unrelenting.

He suggests, again, using the heifer story from Chapter 8. This is basically a lightweight dirty joke, told by Tom to Casy as they're walking home for the first time. A chap called Willy Feely takes a heifer to Graves's bull. Everybody out except the rancher's daughter, Elsie. They put the heifer in the bull's field and sit on the fence to watch. 'Purty soon Willy gets to feelin' purty fly. Elsie looks over, and says, like she don' know, "What's a-matter?" "God," says Willy, "I wish I was doin' what that bull's doin'." An' Elsie says, "Why not? It's your heifer." ' Well. Mildly funny when I first read it, I suppose.

There's also a piece in Chapter 12, a play on the word service, as used in commerce and in mating cattle: 'when I hear a businessman talkin' about service, I wonder who's gettin' screwed.' Marginally more subtle, at least.

Another recommendation is the Happy Hooligan anecdote from Chapter 26, a story told by Tom about a potential escaper from McAlester who was caught the moment he'd scaled the wall. Distraught by failure, he cut his wrists.

I put the heifer story at the end of Act One, Scene Four, after the family huddle, for Al to tell Tom about himself. I'm none too sure about it, but it does give us a moment between the two brothers, makes it clear that Al thinks of himself as a bit of a lad but wants to prove himself to his elder brother. It could also make a point about Tom if, instead of laughing, all boys together, he only smiles and chides Al for getting too big for his boots.

The 'service' quip I give to Casy in Act One, Scene Six, after they've bought new tyres for the Hudson.

The Happy Hooligan story's not going in. How can Rob think it is anything else than utterly bleak?

I write in the one-legged whore story from Chapter 16, giving it to Tom to tell Casy when they meet again after Casy's release from prison, at night outside Hooper's ranch. Here, Casy is urging Tom to tell the peach-pickers inside that as soon as the strike outside the wire is broken, the rate will be cut by half. Tom replies that the workers are downtrodden, sullen, and silent, but they are being paid and would not easily give up their jobs. Someone in jail, he says, told him a story about a one-legged whore who made a virtue of her incapacity and had many satisfied clients.

The story in this context doesn't have the same symbolic meaning as it does in the novel, where it occurs in the One-Eye car wrecking-yard episode. Tom uses it to draw a parallel between the prostitute's clients and the workers at Hooper's: 'People is thinkin' they're jus' purty dam' lucky.'

Casy counters with his 'tell ya what this fella in jail said ta me' speech. If you work for something, you may suffer setbacks, but nevertheless you are always moving forward: 'the only thing you gotta look for is that ever' time they's a li'l step forward, she may slip back a li'l, but she never slips clear back. That means, whatever you do, there's never any waste.'

I'm putting the one-legged whore story into a 'someone told me in jail' context so that Tom and Casy will now be able to swap a jail parable, tell each other something in a way that is both private and significant to themselves. Thus they have a shared bond, they reach an equality at this crucial moment in the play immediately before Casy is killed. It is this bond, and not unchannelled violence, that pushes Tom into killing the guard who murders the preacher.

Monday 18   Re-writes. Decide to lose the 'chicken blood' speech. It's taken from Chapter 22 of the novel, when Ma and Pa are at Weedpatch. Tom has found work. Ma reminisces about what has happened to the family so far, ending with her memory of home, the kitchen door open, and on the table 'the choppin' board with a feather caught on it, all criss-crossed with cuts and black with chicken blood'.

The thing is, I've been seduced by the image and the speech and over the past few months I've shoved it about from one part of the play to another, from Weedpatch, to Needles, to the boxcars, jagging it into scenes like the wrong key into a lock. And it doesn't fit. Pa's following speech about seeing the ducks flying and winter coming on, is in the boxcar scene where it works fine. But not 'chicken blood'. So it went into the bin today.

A lesson learned, though. Everybody working on this play is likely to have their favourite lines or scenes or whatever in the novel, and are going to be looking for them in the play, and probably try to persuade me to put them in if they're not there. But the book's the book, the play's the play. I'm not going to allow my arm to be twisted over somebody's favourite line if it doesn't fit.

Friday 22 According to Duncan, Hal Easton is supposed to be in Edinburgh this week, and I was going to give him the re-writes to take back to America with him, rather than post them. Left messages at the theatre and Royal Scots Club, but no response. So this afternoon, I post a large packet to New York. An hour later, phone rings. Hal.

He comes round to the flat in the evening, eyes flashing, full of news about his 'PR'. Each of the hundreds of theatre companies appearing in Edinburgh during the Festival plasters every reasonably conspicuous city-centre surface with their posters. It's good if you can get a shop to put one up inside their window (weatherproof, people can't poster over you, etc.), but not so much use if there's so many in there already you're elbowed into the top left-hand corner. The Assembly Rooms windows are such a debris of posters nothing stands out at all. Hal, perching on the edge of our sofa and looking like the schoolboy who's won all the prizes, has just rented the Reader's Digest shop-window only two doors along George Street from the Assembly Rooms, exclusively for AFT posters and promotional material.

Part of this promotional material is a series of black-and-white photographs of 1930s dustbowl America, taken for *Time-Life Magazine* and now owned by the US Archive at the Library of Congress in Washington. This sounds very exciting. An exhibition of contemporary photo-journalism must help generate interest in the play.

He has organised the first batch of Press releases on the company's repertoire and these are being mailed to 250 UK and US arts journalists, radio and TV stations, magazines, newspapers . . . The eyes flare up even brighter. He bunches a fist, jabs. 'We just got to get out there, shoot a few crows, see if any fall.'

He leaves, fire-crackering with plans.

Monday 25   We're famous on the streets of Chicago. A name in the windy city. In other words, Steppenwolf know we're in business, presumably from AFT holding auditions. McIntosh and Otis, the American lawyers representing the Steinbeck Estate, have gently reminded Adline Finlay of the maximum number of performances permitted by our release. Perhaps at Steppenwolf's behest or not, I don't know. Wish I knew who was writing Steppenwolf's version. One thing I am prepared to lay a moneyless bet on, in fact do so with Duncan tonight, is that someone representing Steppenwolf will come over and see the play. Wonder if they'll announce themselves or not.

Thursday 28   Have a look at Janet Scarfe's set design. There's been a lot of to-ing and fro-ing about who's going to design *The Grapes* and where the designs are going to be done. The Americans initially thought of having designs made in New York and British stage hands building them here under the supervision of a British technical director, who would also oversee the conversion of the Royal Scots Club basement into a theatre. What this entails is the buying or hiring of stage rostra, scaffolding for a lighting rig, sound and lighting boxes, seats, everything.

The final plan – or current plan which looks as though it will probably be final – is that Janet Scarfe will design *The Grapes* (and three of the other four shows in the AFT repertoire, Lanford Wilson's *Hot l Baltimore*, the Ferber and Kaufman 1930s comedy, *Stage Door*, and Jon Jory's revue, *University*), and also act as technical director.

Janet has worked extensively in several theatres, and with Alan Ayckbourn at the Stephen Joseph Theatre in Scarborough. Her designs are always thoroughly researched and detailed, her best having a strong feel for texture and colour. She has a marked painterly influence which might suit *The Grapes* very well.

A lot of set models look impressive, or rather, dressed up, complete in themselves, card and balsa-wood works of art. This one doesn't. It looks coarse, workmanlike. Obviously, it's carefully contrived, but there's a freedom and spontaneity about it which hopefully won't be lost.

Across a black backcloth, rough-edged, dark ochre receding stripes are painted stage floor to waist level, suggesting furrowed fields, layers of dust, landscape reaching to the horizon. On either side of the stage, a couple of old trunks, a few small wooden boxes and casks, covered with large tarpaulin squares coloured mossy greens and dry-earth shades, represent closer landscape. Uncovered, they'll become the Joads' meagre belongings; moved and covered again, different places on the journey. A six-by-three-foot scrubbed wooden table upstage right symbolises the domesticity of the Joad home, and – the *Nicholas Nickleby* influence – turned upside down, the family sitting on tiers made with the trunks and boxes, the truck. During Act Two, the large table is upstage centre, lengthways on its side. A smaller table is used for Persky's address. Tom's culvert scene is played stage right in a convenient alcove built into the theatre. During the boxcar sequence, Rose of Sharon lies on an old mattress just left of centre stage, the Joad table representing a section of boxcar wall. For the barn, the table is flipped through 180 degrees on to its other side, to reveal the Starving Man lying behind it, the Barn Boy close by.

A very perceptive idea of Janet's: in Act One, Scene Two, Tom, entering stage right, stops and sees Casy for the first time sitting left of stage centre, leaning against a tarpaulin-covered box, lazily singing to himself. In Act Two, Tom plays the culvert scene in almost the same stage-right position and Rose of Sharon's mattress is in the same spot as Casy was. So, we establish a visual thematic link: Tom–Casy; Tom–Rose of Sharon.

On the whole, I'm very pleased. Scene changes – mostly moving stuff about – can be accomplished swiftly by the actors in full view of the audience while other things are happening, in line with the fast-flowing, open, ensemble conventions of the play. I'm worried, though, that whatever we do with lighting, the backdrop will create an exaggerated effect of darkness in a studio theatre, as if it's permanent night out there in the mid-west. Janet says that Rob voiced a similar doubt after she sent him the plans, but that the walls and stage floor in the theatre are black, and that audiences accept the idea of the theatre as a black-box. Besides, we have to have a backdrop to mask a bad wall, and the design budget is not unlimited. Quite the reverse, in fact. I'm not entirely convinced, but the rawness and naturalness of it, the unclutteredness of it, I do like. A studio theatre is a place for actors, not extravagant designs.

JUNE

Tuesday 2   The General Election in nine days'
time. Go tonight to hear Mrs Thatcher speak, what's called a Maggie
Rally, at George Watson's College, a vast, intimidating private school in
an expensive Edinburgh suburb. The big political speeches are ticket-
only affairs and getting tickets, a marathon beginning at my local Tory
campaign office, a former betting shop, took several phone calls and
doubtless a lot of checking up at Conservative Headquarters as to who I
was or, more likely, who I wasn't.

Fierce rain. Hundreds queue down Watson's gravelled drive, a
Roman defence of golfing umbrellas, and shuffle slowly forward
through one side of a double door, through airport security barriers,
through detector beams, past police and dogs, before being thrust into a
heaving jostle of people who must have arrived before the doors opened.
It's as crushed as the floor of the Stock Exchange. In fact, most of the
over-eager young men and braying girls who shove fistfuls of blue paper
hats, postcard-size photographs of Mrs Thatcher, and sheets of lapel
stickers ('We all say YES to Maggie' and 'It's Grr-r-reat to be Great
Again' over a picture of a snarling bulldog) into your hands and actually
into your pockets, might well have been flown up at the close of trading.

Through this gauntlet of reverse-mugging into the hall itself. On a
huge powder-blue stage at the far end a jazz band in glaring pastel
waistcoats bangs diligently through 'Jerusalem', rounding it off with a
discordant squawk. Crowd claps, stamps, waves miniature Union Jacks.
Behind us, heavyweight roadies in tee-shirts check a sound desk as big
as a flight deck. The silver-haired and sober-suited among us, with their
coiffured wives, ill at ease with the whole jamboree, rubber-neck around
the banner-draped balconies for people they know, people who, like
them, thought they ran Edinburgh's entrenched, well-heeled Conservative Party.

Suddenly the lights turn gothic green and dry ice seeps from the
stage. Crowd applauds. Then the lights snap off. We are applauding
total darkness. Identical videos swell up on two huge screens: Maggie,
wearing a headscarf, Boadicea in the turret of a tank; wearing a hard hat,
staring uncertainly at a construction site; hatless, shaking the hands of
world leaders. Simultaneously, Andrew Lloyd Webber's campaign
theme erupts massively and green laser beams splutter and whirl over
our heads, scribbling *Maggie makes it three* in mid-air. Audience, on its

feet, bays and howls. Just as suddenly, this hideous spectacle stops and the lights come on the audience, many of whom are now wearing their paper hats and their little stickers. An embarrassed party official, grinning like a northern club comic, haltingly introduces the Prime Minister. Flag-waving uproar as a small, permed, blue-suited woman clutching a large, old-fashioned handbag emerges from the wings. In front of me, two immensely pretty girls shriek and bob, cascading ringlets of hair shaking over their shoulders.

The speech is banal, delivered in an inexorable monotone which only stops, possibly at places already marked in the script, to cue the applause which duly comes.

Nobody heckles. Nobody is likely to. A TV news programme the other night showed a heckler muscled out of a Kinnock rally, a rally that looked no less blatantly stage-managed than this. Politics is a sales pitch now, orchestrated by marketing and advertising agencies, and these shindigs are for those who have already bought in.

At the end, crowd hysterical. Mrs Thatcher bows, steps back, steps forward, bows again. I feel an intruder, marooned, like the journalist James Penfield in the film, *The Ploughman's Lunch*. The party flunkey, still stupidly bovine, announces that, as the band plays 'Land of Hope and Glory', 'Mrs Thatcher will pass among you'. Crowd stands again and thumps along in time as, surrounded by a mobile barrier of TV lights and security staff, a small waving hand does a circuit of the hall. Occasionally, a glimpse of the face below it, its jaw locked into a rictus smile, its powder flaking in the heat. The sober-suits lean forward, thrusting hands through the cordon like so many Falstaffs trying to catch the benediction of the newly-crowned Henry V. The Union Jacks wave and fly, the band blasts, the girls leap and jig. They, others like them, and the male paper-hat distributors, have walkie-talkies clipped to their belts. The hired cheerleaders, the sleek men, the perky girls, front-line troops in the open, callous manipulation of politics. But as the banners sway and the music plays, who really notices or cares? The roadies are pulling the plugs already. Tomorrow, another city, another show.

Tuesday 9   The Tony Awards on TV. Most of the winners – all announced to tumultuous applause – read laboriously from prepared lists of people to thank, in more cases than one everybody from their children to their God with apologies to anyone missed out. Others oozed unctuousness. 'Oh, thank you for loving my work!' yelled a middle-aged actress who looked as though she was wrapped in aluminium foil. Perhaps TV made the total absence of humility, the avarice, the deep, deep need to win prizes, more disturbing than it really was. Perhaps.

Friday 12   Mrs Thatcher wins as convincingly as it always looked she would. On TV, the Party Chairman, Norman Tebbit, lurks outside Conservative Central Office or somewhere, holding an enormous bunch of red roses that he thrusts into the Prime Minister's arms with a ghastly smile. As the Labour Party symbol is a red rose, they look like floral John the Baptist heads. The chap fitting my new gas-cooker stops to watch admiringly.

'She's sorted the Gas Board out alright,' says this new small shareholder. 'Productivity.' His hand swoops upwards. 'You wouldn't believe it.'

Wednesday 24   One of Hal's crows has fallen: *The Grapes* is listed in *The Independent* today as one of the shows to look out for at the Festival. Admittedly, one of a selection of about fifty, but to be one of fifty from a choice of several hundred is encouraging, and one of the advantages of alphabetical order is the company name is near the top of the column. We're listed twice (under American Festival Theatre and Netherbow Theatre), in the Fringe Programme, also out this week, a fat, A4-size free magazine listing plays, cabarets, revues, concerts, exhibitions – well over 500 companies producing about 850 events in 130 venues. An unattributed quote below our first entry: 'A major theatrical event.'

In *The Independent*, we're listed after 'Prime Venues', the Assembly Rooms, Traverse Theatre, Richard Demarco Gallery. One problem anyone not performing at these venues is going to have is persuading the more important critics to come to their productions. Even well-established writers and directors like Richard Crane and Faynia Williams, who have regularly won *Scotsman* Fringe First Awards, have come up against this creeping critical myopia.

The Assembly Rooms has by far the biggest concentration of events, international theatre, and current big names from TV comedy, and the Traverse has a reputation of innovative theatre behind it. In my opinion, well behind it. In its early days, in the 1960s and 1970s, it was the centre of the Fringe and an influential theatre the rest of the year. But lately its directors have buried it in a swamp of self-indulgent, over-written and badly-acted historical fantasy. The place swallows a vast amount of Arts Council money, is only open part of each year and the core of its August Festival programming is now a re-run of plays produced there from April to July. The Demarco Gallery is a maverick. Much of what is on each year is mediocre, but there is always something unmissable and Richard Demarco himself is Edinburgh's true iconoclast. Cosmopolitan, intensely industrious, his fervent championship of what he believes in makes him an essential and invigorating Festival presence.

So, it is possible for major newspapers to 'cover' the Fringe simply by their critics shuttling between these three, but it's hardly a deep trawl and a miserable reflection of the spirit of the thing. The size of choice at Assembly is persuasive and sentimental attachment keeping the Traverse afloat dies hard, especially with rising ticket prices. Once you could take a chance on something unknown at a church hall and turn up a pearl for 75p. And if you found it to be paste, well, 75p wasn't too great a stake to lose. But at £3.50 (the average, and what we're charging for *The Grapes*), people not surprisingly want some sort of guarantee. What is vital to any company is good word-of-mouth, and everyone can rely on being reviewed in *The Scotsman*, the most important newspaper at Festival time.

Nevertheless, the Netherbow is a good venue. A well-designed and fully-equipped theatre with good seating, on the High Street midway between the Castle and Holyrood Palace, surrounded by designer knitwear shops, which means a potential audience is always passing the doors.

Friday 26   The first AFT Press pack. Press bumf is important. From now on every arts journalist in Britain will be inundated with the stuff, so yours has to stand out but not be so pushy it gets up people's noses. Press material is starting to cascade through my letterbox every day and it ranges from the unreadable, either literally so because it's murkily Xeroxed on grey, pulpy paper, or because whoever has written it is apparently illiterate, to agency-designed card folders with full-colour pull-out posters, free programmes, the works. And everybody, even the illiterate, has scraped a glowing quote from somewhere.

AFT's comes in a natty plastic folder, the blurb adorned by a pen drawing for *The Grapes*, a dungareed man standing on a road, a swirl of dust across the skyline. Full of rosy American prose.

Grapes Three, the rehearsal script, arrives from New York. All the cuts cut, the re-writes inserted, the whole thing typed, proofread, corrected, copied, and distributed to us and our still unknown cast whose names now appear on the title page.

Am I pleased with it? Yes. With conditions. It's not the final script, of course. I'll probably be re-writing up to the opening but with luck not beyond it. Duncan is far less happy about this than I am, but I'm looking forward to working as part of a larger team, to walking to, and about, a rehearsal room after months of sitting at a desk. So now is the time, if any, for a moment alone with it, so to speak, pat its back, wish it luck. An about-to-be-produced play. Fully cast. With the exception of Barn Boy . . .

The script is the shortest yet. In fact, the first draft of the second act was longer than the whole play is now – Act One is 38 pages, Act Two 40, a total of 78.

The running order, oddly enough, is almost unchanged: Act One, Scene One – short cameos of Tom, Tenant, Tractor Man, Used-Car Salesman; Scene Two – Tom meeting Casy; Scene Three – homecoming; Scene Four – family huddle, decisions, heifer story; Scene Five – Ma and Tom, Tom: 'You jus' gotta take ever' day as she comes'; Scene Six – Granma refusing to leave, the road, Connie and Rose of Sharon besotted by Oklahoma City, the Wilsons, death of Granma, the Wilsons and Joads going on together; Scene Seven – the road, Gas-Station Man; Scene Eight – Connie's big plans for the future, Wilsons' car breaks down, and Ma threatens Pa with jack-handle when he agrees they carry on while Tom fixes it; Scene Nine – Colorado River bank, Casy and homegoing Texan; Scene Ten – Noah leaving, Joads setting out across desert leaving Wilsons behind; Scene Eleven – the desert, Rose of Sharon and Connie love-making prelude, California.

Act Two, Scene One – Persky and Bird, Floyd, arrest of Casy at Hooverville, Connie leaves; Scene Two – Weedpatch, Wallace, Mrs Thomas; Scene Three – prelude to dance, Old Woman and Rose of Sharon; Scene Four – Tom, Al, Higgins; Scene Five – Ma and Pa confrontation, decision that Joads leave; Scene Six – Casy outside Hooper's Ranch; Scene Seven – Tom meets Casy outside Hooper's, Casy killed; Scene Eight – inside Joad hut at Hooper's, Rose of Sharon taunts Tom with having killed again, Ma decides the family must leave and move on; Scene Nine – to the boxcars; Scene Ten – the boxcars,

Aggie and Al; Scene Eleven – boxcar, Rose of Sharon's confession, Tom and Ma at the culvert, the stillbirth, flood; Scene Twelve – the barn.

A letter from Albert. Wants Granma's religiosity written in. 'Hillbilly,' mutters Duncan. They've misinterpreted the one-legged whore story, but that'll be easy enough to sort out once they're here. A couple of other quibbles, nothing major.

That's it, then. Phase One finished. Phase Two about to start.

Sunday 28   Dip into the play, deliberately minus pen and notebook so I don't start tinkering here and there. Although Old Woman–dance and Al and Aggie sequences need a complete de-coke and overhaul, and I want to build Connie and Rose of Sharon more in rehearsals, other bits stand up. Ma, Pa, Casy, Noah all look secure. Discovered a cut in Act Two, Scene Five, the entire page 55, which should have been, but has not, been cut by the New York typist. All to the good, really. It'll give me something to contribute when I face the first read-through on Monday week.

JULY

Saturday 4   London. The cast scheduled to arrive today. US Independence Day.

With Vivien to Her Majesty's Theatre, where Andrew Lloyd Webber's musical, *The Phantom of the Opera*, is playing. She is recording an interview with James Paterson before the matinée for the BBC Radio Scotland arts programme she works on.

James Paterson's is a wonderful story. After eleven years mostly in the chorus and understudying at Scottish Opera, he's landed two baritone roles, Don Attilio and Passarino, in excerpts from operas performed at the Paris Opera House in the show, roles he cheerfully describes as 'two-liners'.

But he hurtled to prominence, literally overnight, at the end of April when Michael Crawford, playing the Phantom, was taken ill.

'On the Tuesday afternoon, I had a phone call saying that Michael Crawford was in hospital, that Steve Barton (Raoul) would be playing the Phantom, that David Firth would also be moving into another role and as his understudy, I would be playing his part, Monsieur Andre, the Opera House manager. Steve Barton, however, had hurt his leg rehearsing earlier in the afternoon, but he got through the show that night. I'm second Phantom understudy and next day, Wednesday, I was asked to come in early as it seemed that Steve Barton might only be able to play the matinée and I would have to do the evening performance. But at lunchtime, the news came that Michael Crawford had discharged himself from hospital and he played both performances. But on Thursday, he was back in hospital and wasn't to be allowed out. Steve Barton was having medical treatment to his leg and so by 2 o'clock I was in the theatre, rehearsing to play the Phantom that night.'

The story hit every newspaper – after all, the show's sold out until March next year and every day there's a queue for returns outside the theatre. On his first night, he had a congratulatory telephone call from Andrew Lloyd Webber in France and a huge ovation from the audience, something he modestly glosses over.

'The understudy's job is (a) to know the words, (b) to know the music, (c) to know the geography of the production, so you can fill the gaps and the rest of the cast can perform as they normally do. All that goes without saying. But, most important, the audience have paid for a performance and that is what you must give. I can't be Michael Crawford. I'm not a mimic, the sort of person who can instantly switch to being someone else. That's not the job at all. The job is to give your own performance. So when I watched the show on the Wednesday afternoon, I wasn't watching Michael Crawford so much as the role itself.'

During his years with Scottish Opera, he says, 'nothing much was happening. In Glasgow I never really believed that I could get to London. But I'm here now and very happy.'

The queue that was outside the foyer doors at midday by 2.30 snakes around the building as far as the stage door. At its head a myopic, puddingy young woman in a Phantom tee-shirt and a spindly, anaemic-looking man sit in garden chairs and appear to be organising everyone else, darting into the crowd every now and then. Revealing badly aligned teeth, and clutching a vacuum flask, she says she 'works here'.

'What as?'

'Well,' with a glance into the foyer, 'not officially. But I look after the queue. You know.' Leaning forward, she adds confidingly that today is her twenty-first anniversary.

'Anniversary of what?'

Of seeing the show. After today, she'll have seen it on average twice a month. It turns out she queues almost daily, sometimes for tickets, sometimes 'just to . . .' She peers at someone in the queue. 'You know.' Just being here, being part of this crowd, persuading herself and anyone who listens that she has some influence in it, is very important to her. There's three or four others like her, all of whom appear a little odd in some way. Acutely lonely, probably. 'I've seen Andrew Lloyd Webber,' she says. 'Oh, yeah. Once sat in one of the seats he keeps reserved. You know.'

Another girl, fifth in the queue, small and pretty, isn't queuing for herself although she comes here almost every day as well. She queues for other people, mostly American tourists in twos, charging one pound per ticket per hour. She reckons to make £16 today and hopes to see *Melon* over the road tonight.

'Them paying me's cheaper than going to the black market,' she says.

It is. I went to a commercial ticket agency as an experiment and the chap behind the counter went through a well-rehearsed theatrical routine of disbelief that I was naïve enough to think tickets were actually available.

'But what I can do,' he said, swivelling about to make sure nobody was listening, then staring past my left ear and muttering confidentially, 'is see about laying me hands on a couple for tomorrow. Hundred pounds each.'

The show itself is a savage disappointment. It is beautifully lit, Maria Bjornson's sets, descending bridges, candelabras rising through dry-ice underground lakes, and grey Parisian roofscapes recall nineteenth-century transformation scenes with little conspicuous twentieth-century gadgetry. It is not, at least, a computer musical. But the libretto is woefully insubstantial and the music itself, a carapace of bludgeoning, simplistic melodies given lush orchestration, is emotionally void. It has no heart whatever. The show tells you nothing about humanity and left me coldly unmoved. The night belongs to the set designer and to Michael Crawford, who sings well and invests the Phantom with a character, dignity, sympathy, and depth noticeably absent from the music.

Monday 6   To International Hall in Blooms-bury for the first read-through, scheduled for 9 a.m. Arrive at quarter to. A large, old, tattered building full of cheap rooms for touring students and teachers. Piles of linen waiting for laundry collection dumped in the linoleumed lobby, a smell of coffee and frying evidently from a lower floor communal breakfast room, metal lift doors juddering open and closed, inhaling and exhaling groups of people, almost all of whom carry bags of some shape and form. Hal, whisking past almost at a run, calls 'hi' and says something about having come from a breakfast meeting before disappearing around a corner.

Get Rob's room number from a glum-looking porter mooching about behind the reception desk and take a lift, straining on its haulage gear and clanging in its shaft, to the fourth floor. On the way, attempted to adopt a look of professional composure, but felt only a conflict of rigid apprehension and bullish defensiveness, not being able to think what professional composure might look like anyway.

Found Rob ambling along the corridor to his hired read-through room, in neat jeans, sneakers, and red sweatshirt, sleeves pulled up to elbows, looking, in other words, professionally composed, the effect of which was to make me feel even more agitated. The script under my arm feels suddenly at its most insubstantial; perhaps I should have beefed it up a bit on the tube.

By 9, fifteen actors have arranged themselves in a horseshoe of chairs

78

abutting a long table at which I sit next to Rob. On the far side of him, Jodi Klosner, the assistant director, and alongside her, a corn-haired woman whose name I didn't catch, the costume designer wearing designer clothes.

Both the room and the day outside are sweat-hot already and the windows are fully open to the thunder of traffic beating its way through inert air from Brunswick Square below. The actors sit silently, patiently waiting for something to happen. From a quick glance around I see that some have their scripts impressively ring-bindered; others have them still as loose pages in the envelopes in which they were sent. But Rob has cast excellently, for age at least: Dorothy Bernard, eccentrically dressed in khaki shorts and white blouson jacket, thin and frail and in her seventies, is right for Granma; Albert and Faith Geer, both possibly in their fifties, are well suited as Ma and Pa, Faith having the strong, sturdy build of a woman raised on the land. George McGrath, tall, lean, grey-haired, quiet, looks a perfect Preacher Casy, and the younger company members fresh-faced and sharp.

Rob, an unused spiral-bound notebook open in front of him, pencil and tube of mints at a precise right angle beside it, makes a speech about this being the world premiere of the first authorised stage version of *Grapes*, privilege of working on it, script a working script and therefore as with any new play subject to change and development, all heard the one about the song that stops the show only being given to the actors the day of opening night, weeks ahead of continual and communal exploration, discovering text and characters, great responsibility. Then announced first change to the script, something I'd just told him about, the cutting of page 55, which we had agreed to cut in May, but which the typist in New York had inadvertently not cut from the final copy. Fortuitously, as it turned out, because it meant that everyone could flip pages, repeat the page number aloud, confer, cross out, check their neighbour's script against their own, repeat aloud the new succeeding lines, and generally create a bustle of activity, an illusion of work being done, decisions made, script actually being developed on the first day, the subsequent read-through being a minor matter of course.

Finally, Peter Spears mumbled his way into Tom's first speech, Albert took up Pa's . . . and into the small cameo sections at the beginning of the play intended to quickly sketch a portrait of America and the 1930s. It began to feel to me, listening to these hesitant words, like wading through waist-high mud. From out of the dead air floated a voice reading like an old recording of Gielgud giving a soliloquy from

Hamlet, but a New York version in which sentences and even words were broken haphazardly, even wilfully. This extraordinary rendition shimmered in and out of audibility probably in time with the traffic lights changing somewhere below, giving the reading an even more surreal quality than it had already.

But once into Act One, Scene Two, the meeting of Casy and Tom, we hit surer ground. George almost knows his lines already and reads simply but with conviction, his torso hunched over the script on his knees. Peter, sitting at his feet, visibly relaxes and for a moment something of a Tom–Casy relationship seems to flicker.

Most of the read-through I spend head slumped forward like a hanged, but sitting, man, staring at my script, occasionally sneaking glances upwards. Rob sits passively chewing. If some sections seem to flow, others already show signs of problems: the opening of the Weedpatch scene is a particularly forced transposition, the dance sequence is difficult to tell but sounded lumpish and lifeless, there are clumps and tangles all over the place that have to be weeded out. The Al and Aggie interchange, at present only eight lines long, is virtually meaningless. Albert was right – there has to be much more in there. Albert was right on another point, too – there isn't enough humour. Huge sections at the moment drag menacingly, like a man in chains making his way laboriously to join me on my sedentary scaffold.

We finish. Nobody, at least, makes a dash to the airport. Rob passes around some Xeroxed photographs of dustbowl America. Powerful images of natural assault and ruin: wooden, single-storey houses, little more than large sheds, disappearing behind huge, swirling clouds of earth dust; a father chasing a toddler across a patch of wilderness, the child obliterated by dust as though running madly into cannon smoke; bewildered, huddled families in incongruous straw hats; men standing self-consciously beside ageing trucks sagging on their axles beneath the weight of bedsteads, chairs, tables, meagre family possessions looking all the more pathetic when piled hurriedly together; dogs, thin and bent-backed; children, mawkish in the stifling heat.

Finally, we go around the room, introducing ourselves. It becomes not merely a name-check, but in places one of those American group sessions, one or two revealing as matter-of-factly as if they were discussing their travel arrangements, intimate details of their personal and emotional lives. This causes no surprise whatever to the others. Americans have a disarming, and sometimes chilling, habit of speaking entirely openly to absolute, or comparative, strangers in a way that most

British people wouldn't, even to their closest friends. But for Americans it creates a – naïve perhaps, genuine maybe – security, a comfort within a group. And the group receives these mini-confessions respectfully, even gratefully, something to be remembered.

A second thing, a real surprise to me, is that they regard appearing in commercials and industrial training films as legitimate acting credits, an activity British actors might do to pay the rent but would not regard as a positive career step. But most have stage credits, some of them impressive: George McGrath has several seasons of New York Shakespeare behind him and has worked extensively with Richard Foreman. Paul Binotto, playing Connie, has appeared in *Sweeney Todd* with New York City Opera, in *Dreamgirls*, and has just left the Broadway production of *Starlight Express* to do *The Grapes of Wrath*. Faith has several film credits, others have off-Broadway and regional credits in Chicago and elsewhere. It looks like an interesting, and hopefully fertile mix from extensive experience through to comparative inexperience. At which end of the scale I place myself.

Later: National Theatre – *Fathers and Sons*, Brian Friel's adaptation of Turgenev, in the Lyttelton. Internal smoulderings of love, external proclamations of nihilism during summer at provincial family villa. Chekhovian rhythms, first act heavy with exposition. Friel's writing makes the play rather remote. Wonder why Arkady is given equal dramatic weight with Yevgeny, rather than being used as a narrator figure. The scattering of contemporary phrases strikes bizarre notes, and would a young male Russian servant in 1859 have 'multi-coloured hair' and a turquoise ear-ring? An urge to reach for the novel, not from excitement, from doubt.

Tuesday 7   Royal Court director Simon Curtis's account of his recent trip to see American theatre, in *Plays Magazine*. Steppenwolf in rehearsal for *Aunt Dan and Lemon* – their current production is Sam Shepard's *A Lie of the Mind*. '*Lie* here seems soggy and vague. The real talent in this company seems to have left for the movies.'

Interesting.

Wednesday 8   To the Shaftesbury Theatre, to record a radio interview with Dolores Gray, the American star of Stephen
Sondheim's *Follies*, opening in a couple of weeks time.

She is, according to Albert, 'the essence of the Broadway musical'.
She starred as Annie in the first London production of *Annie Get Your
Gun* in 1947, returned to play Rose in *Gypsy* in 1974, and is now
rehearsing Carlotta Campion in *Follies*.

She leads the way from the stage door, grumbling at the flights of
stone steps, across the stage fenced by scaffolding and swathed in
polythene sheeting (in the show, Weismann's theatre is to be de-
molished the next day), to a small bar behind the stalls. Her forearms
jangle with bangles, her head is topped by a regal swirl of blonde hair.
She is a commanding presence and, I imagine, enjoys being the great
star that she is.

The greatest Broadway score: '*Follies* is certainly one of them. There
are some brilliant things in it. I think *Gypsy* is one of the greatest scores
ever written. Stephen Sondheim wrote the lyrics, Jule Styne the music.'

The archetypical Broadway composer: 'Stephen Sondheim. His
works stand quite apart because he doesn't simply write 32-bar songs.
He takes all the skeins, all the silks and weaves a whole piece that
furthers the show. That is what a musical is about; some of the emotions
the characters are feeling are sung. And they used to be sung in a
straightforward, standard kind of *Annie Get Your Gun* way, because
Irving Berlin was that kind of writer. He wrote a 32-bar song, and wrote
you five choruses of the same 32 bars, with funny little lyrics . . .
Wonderful songs. But the style has gone forward now. It's gone deeper
and wider so that in Sondheim you cannot just pull one song out,
because if you did, it wouldn't be just a song that was missing but an
emotional bridge from one scene to the next. He has lifted the musical
from *Annie* and *Kiss Me Kate* on to a whole other plane.'

Thursday 9   National Theatre: *A Small Family
Business*, the new Alan Ayckbourn play in the Olivier. It is a contemporary morality tale, how honest Jack McCracken, taking over the family
furniture business, becomes sucked into a mire of petty, then dangerous, corruption. The exterior of the play is farce – and farce, used by a
master like Ayckbourn, points to an interior of anguish, even tragedy.
Each play of Ayckbourn's is becoming more extreme in form and
content. While wildly funny, they're deeply understanding and very
serious.

Saturday 11   Haymarket Theatre Royal: Simon
Gray's new play, *Melon*. A study of a successful publisher's mental
collapse, precipitated by his both wanting and not wanting to know the
name of his wife's lover. An outstanding performance of jittery tension
by Alan Bates as Mark Melon, a man so at the centre of, and so
dominant in, his world, a competitor so accustomed to winning the
prizes, that when that world's symmetry suddenly breaks, when he
begins to lose, he disintegrates completely.

But what worries me is the sequence in which Melon, in a kind of
hallucination, is confronted by the males he suspects and taunted by his
wife, an echoey chorus of 'cuckold' swinging around the theatre. Within
seconds the scene falls on its face, out for the count, partly because of
some mechanical knob-twiddling that makes everyone's voice except
Melon's sound like Donald Duck. Now, the comparison in tone
between this and the Old Woman–Rose of Sharon scene in *The Grapes* is
pretty tenuous, so tenuous as to hardly exist, probably, but dramatically
the cuckold scene, the only one like it in the play, is nevertheless more of
the fabric of *Melon* than the Old Woman scene, again the only one like
it, is of *The Grapes*, and if cuckold patently doesn't work, then Old
Woman has an even rougher ride ahead of it than I imagined.

I'm becoming rather jittery myself.

Monday 13   First day of rehearsal. I've pre-
arranged with Rob not to go, not wholly out of fear, but possibly implied
a slightly more zealous concern than I actually feel that the cast should
acclimatise themselves to Edinburgh, find their way about, generally
settle down with each other and the play, and that it would be easier for
them to do this if I wasn't at rehearsal to start with. Duncan, having just
moved into a new office to run his theatre administration consultancy, is
reluctant to go to rehearsals at all.

Consequently, spend most of the morning pacing about at home,
flipping through the play occasionally, wondering what they're up to. At
lunchtime, hunt out Duncan in his sub-basement office and work off a
bit of nervousness by pacing about, flipping, wondering, etc., etc. Leave
him probably with frazzled nerves and meander along to the Royal Scots
Club not far away. Upstairs, in a dining room of true Scottish spacious-
ness and oppressiveness, the forty-strong AFT company sit like school-
children around a huge square table with a grim and parsimonious
centrepiece of one cruet and a sauce bottle, eating meat that looks like

the soles of well-worn shoes and mashed potato.

The five AFT directors, and Albert, the schoolmasters, have a table by themselves. Rob, looking grateful to abandon his plate, and I, have a chat about rehearsals: come along any time I like, not before Saturday; re-capitulate lines of communication: all ideas from cast *re* script changes to go to Rob, then Duncan and myself, discuss three-way, Rob takes decisions back; all ideas from us go to Rob, discuss three-way, Rob takes to cast.

Our first three-way script meeting is on Thursday.

Thursday 16   Script meeting with Rob and Albert in Hal's office at the top of the Royal Scots Club, Albert sitting managerially at the desk, Rob, Duncan, and myself on hard chairs in front of it, Albert methodically laying out his script and notes as though checking our credit rating for some sort of loan.

Rob reports that so far at rehearsals he is running the blocking of Act One. What this entails is working through the text with the actors and whatever pieces of stage furniture, trunks, boxes, barrels, and so on, already delivered to the rehearsal room (and not much has arrived yet, small wooden barrels being surprisingly difficult to come by), to find out where each actor should be at any particular moment and who moves where when, in relation to whom and what, to create a visually dramatic but at the same time entirely natural stage dynamic. Although this initial blocking will be revised when each scene is broken down and progressively rehearsed, it means that actors and director are working from the same basis. Meanwhile, the actors are beginning to rehearse without the scripts in their hands.

Long discussion on Granma. Tom doesn't actually say hello to her in front of the audience as he does the rest of the family. Albert is insistent, and Rob highly in favour, that an introductory 'welcome' is written in when Granma first appears, in the Scene Four family huddle. And Albert is equally insistent that Granma does some 'blubbering' and religious glorying as she's dying in Scene Six. At the moment, she is obviously ill, but quiet, an old woman whose spirit has crumbled. One of the pro-blubbering and glorying arguments is that Dorothy Bernard is a very good actress. This, to me, is irrelevant to whether the character should go into histrionics or not. Or is Albert actually trying to reinstate those suggestions of his that I vetoed before, or is Dorothy saying her role is under-written? The point is, Granma's death is important not so much as an event in itself, but in its placing in the play and the effect it has on the rest of the family. Build it into a great operatic display for one actress and we lose the dramatic balance and purpose. And deaths are difficult at the best of times, even more so on a small stage with the audience only six feet away.

Finally agree that Tom should leave the huddle for a moment for a reassuring word with Granma when she enters, but that the death scene is unaltered and emblematic.

Cut one-legged whore story for Act Two. This is a great pity. But it emerged that between the four of us there were four differing interpretations of the story in the context in which I've placed it. Rob, pencil hovering over the lines, adds that on this basis, if we have a full house there could be up to seventy-five differing interpretations of the speech. I concede that would be confusing rather than dramatically interesting so it falls, as did chicken blood, to the blue pencil.

The Barn Boy – or Girl – question is becoming even more complex, as the actress who was playing Aggie Wainwright, who is both petite and looks young enough to get away with Barn Girl as well, has left the cast to replace an actress in another AFT show who had to fly back to the States. Heather Hitt, playing the lead in *Stage Door*, is taking over Aggie but, willowy and porcelain-skinned as she is and looking younger than her 20 years as she does, is still not young enough for Barn Girl. Rob's suggestion is that he persuade George McGrath's young daughter, Miranda, who has accompanied her father to Edinburgh, to play the role. Miranda is small, slim, literally the right age, and while not playing in any AFT show at the moment, is the daughter of actors – George is playing Casy – and has hopes of a stage career herself. Agree that Rob talk to her and George.

An unexpected concern is that Peter Spears, playing Tom Joad, is, according to Rob, not rehearsing nearly as well as he auditioned and appears unsettled in the role. This is surprising to me as he was certainly impressive at the read-through. Still, I'll see when I go to the run of Act One on Saturday.

Albert makes a contribution, orchestrated by a lot of screwing up of eyes and fingers furrowing hair, as to whether it is clear in the play that Oklahoma has not always been a dustbowl but productive farming land. One of the other actors had raised this with him, he was merely passing it on. This apparent early contravention of the cast–Rob–Duncan and myself lines of communication we had laboriously delineated irrationally gets my antennae going. If I had bothered to look at the script properly, I could have pointed out that after Tom's opening, the first line in the play, spoken by the Tenant (now, incidentally, played by Pa Joad and therefore spoken by Albert himself) is 'Ever' year we got a good crop comin' . . .' and the whole scene, in fact, refers to the changed situation, meaning, Oklahoma once productive. End of conversation. Instead, the realisation that it's a bit hypocritical of me to get on a procedural high horse after roughriding over Duncan's sensibilities in March, causes me to waffle. Once the meeting is ended (by Hal muscling his computer, a keyboard the size of a shoebox, a printer the size of a suitcase, into the room – like his calculator-wristwatch, he never goes anywhere without it), I chivvy Rob into the corridor, leaving Albert fiddling with a telephone and muttering about changing his room as he can't sleep, to reiterate cast–director–writers procedure. I am, evidently, none too clear, as Rob keeps nodding and murmuring 'Where is the crux of all this?'

'What Peter means . . .,' chimes in Duncan.

Between us, we work out an approximation of what Peter means, by the end of which it emerges that Peter doesn't mean anything very much except the quite important issue (to me) that Rob, as director, should now be in the driving seat of the play and that Albert, as actor, should be concentrating on rehearsing rather than dramaturgy.

Saturday 18   Sixth day of rehearsal, supposedly a run-through of Act One for lines and blocking. 8.15 a.m., battle out in lancing rain, low mist, November cold, an Edinburgh summer's day, to rehearsals at a church hall on The Pleasance, a road weaving up from the High Street alongside Salisbury Crags, a moonscape of bare earth and grimy rock escarpment on the edge of town. Peter Spears fights his way down the street from the opposite direction and we go in together, closely followed by a figure wearing a dripping, hooded, floor-length green oilskin and looking like a drenched Kermit the Frog but which turns out to be Albert, still worried about his sleep. The rest of the cast arrive, frail Dorothy blown in through the door behind her open umbrella, Chris Ann Moore, playing Rose of Sharon, in a soaked ankle-length dress, incongruously nursing two cans of Coca-Cola.

The hall is unheated, so actors already cold after America and London are even colder, and the other side of town from the Royal Scots Club where all the other shows are being rehearsed – in the warm – and where their lunch is served every day. But rehearsal space in Edinburgh is both limited and, pre-Festival, expensive. The Edinburghers are alive to supply and demand profits and this is the best we could get.

The floor is marked out with masking-tape showing the dimensions of the theatre stage. Rob, benign and quiet, Jodi Klosner, his assistant, and Graham Smith, the production stage manager recruited by Duncan, sit at a line of tables facing the acting area. I slip in beside them.

An odd, spasmodic morning. The actors are subdued, watchful of each other, not working as an ensemble yet because this early in rehearsals everyone is very much on his or her own; some know almost all their lines, others don't and are dependent on having the script in their hands, some are more confident of the blocking than others and frequent stops and restarts make it difficult for them to find any overall sense of flow. Some of the more experienced actors like George McGrath are already tentatively experimenting with performance possibilities while others are concentrating on the rhythms in the text. Both George and Paul Binotto, playing Connie, an experienced Broadway actor, are being careful to create an atmosphere in which the less experienced do not feel inhibited. It is a day to continue establishing mutual trust, to discover progress made, and possible directions to follow rather than analyse results so far. For myself, it is the first chance to look at the play evolving in the round.

First alarm: Casy and Tom in the Scene Two meeting. I'd always conceived of Casy being reserved in this scene, cautiously sounding out Tom with all these theories he has, while Tom is diffident, jokey, not wanting to become too involved. It is played today as almost exactly the reverse. It works, surprisingly, or partly works, although George's Casy veers towards the hand-flapping glory-shouting one moment and abruptly switches to the cosily confidential the next, lunging his body forward, breaking his sentences half-way through and giving a kind of rattling laugh in place of full-stops. It swerves giddily between the fundamentalist harangue and the Brooklyn hang-loose. Peter's Tom, on the other hand, looks taut and intent, as though his mind is preoccupied by concentrating on a long and involved novel. It probably is. *The Grapes of Wrath*.

And after Tom passes Casy his liquor bottle and he takes a swig from it, Casy casually lobs it back, something a man who's been in the wilderness and hasn't had a drink for some time surely would not do, especially to a man who has just spent a buck – a lot of money – on the precious stuff.

But the main thing is the small flame of the Casy–Tom relationship I saw at the read-through is still burning.

Other immediate problems: Damien Kavanagh's Noah. Something very strange here. Brooding presence has become absolutely retarded. He gazes vacantly, rolls his head, allows his tongue on occasion to loll from his mouth. And when he does speak, an American whine comes out, making Noah sound not only retarded but positively camp.

And the death scene looks as though it's written in shorthand. For an important set piece, blink and you miss it. It is not helped by the fact that Granma herself is working without the script and although she appears to know her comparatively few lines, gives no indication of being disposed to say them either in the correct order or at the correct time. The perfunctorious brevity of the whole thing is only emphasised by Connie leading the Joads and Wilsons in an unaccompanied hymn ('Softly, tenderly, Jesus is calling . . .') at her graveside. This is because Paul has a wonderful voice and it carries a genuine emotion that visibly gets to the actors, which Granma's death plainly doesn't. The rendition itself is strongly Mormon Tabernacle Choir, overflowing with descanting harmonies, but that's not the important thing. The important thing is that Albert was right on Thursday. The scene desperately needs building, and needs something in there to create a sense of time passing between Granma's collapse and her death. But not blubbering. Something else.

On we plod. It is clear that Rose of Sharon and Connie are almost disastrously underwritten. Rose of Sharon has a particularly precarious base in Act One from which to emerge as a pivotal, perhaps the pivotal, Act Two character. Connie, the man who leads on this girl-child with his charm and cunning, is hardly registering in the play at all. Everything is being contributed by Paul in the way of looks and glances.

Decide to write more Rose of Sharon and Connie, give them two or three more episodes, unfolding their relationship, placing one episode midway through the death scene to create the time-scale it needs. Talk to Rob about this afterwards. Rob at the moment is like a sponge, absorbing everything, turning nothing down, keeping all options open.

Sunday 19   Work on re-writes, or rather, fresh Rose of Sharon and Connie sequences.

I now realise that my agitation last week, and especially on Thursday, was due to my suddenly feeling that I didn't have a place in this new phase of the process. But being at rehearsal yesterday made me feel an essential component of a team again, or what is now a group of individuals but who will hopefully meld into a team. Partly, I suppose, the feeling is a product of necessity, the play needing a lot more writing work, but it goes deeper than that. Last week I felt a bit left out. Now I don't.

Monday 20   Meet Duncan outside the BBC in Queen Street where he'd just been interviewed on puppet theatre on *The Jimmy Mack Show*, a mid-morning pop, prattle 'n' giggle radio programme. He'd gone on twenty minutes ahead of schedule because the intended previous interviewee, a gardener, hadn't turned up. As he's going on to a meeting in the afternoon to do with his business, Edinburgh Arts Promotions, he's wearing a grey pin-stripe suit, a green-and-white stripe shirt and carrying a briefcase. I, in corduroys, sweater, and script in a carrier bag, complete what must be a vividly contrasting collaboration to present at rehearsal.

Seventh day of rehearsal. Better than Saturday if only because of the weather. Didn't show Rob my new Rose of Sharon and Connie pieces as I want to see another run of what we already have and check what needs to be put where.

Today there is even more stop-starting and revision of blocking and nobody seems any further forward with lines.

The heifer story at the end of Scene Four looks exactly what it is, an appendage shoved in fairly late in the day. We've now tried it both finishing with Tom chiding Al's one-of-the-boys attitude to life, and without, and although the former is marginally better, nothing as it stands integrates the story with what comes before or after it. It occurs to me that as its inclusion was not my idea, whether I've allowed myself to be steam-rollered into accepting it. Have I? Possibly. I have considered a lot of ideas I instinctively felt were wrong for the play, but at the same time I have been insistent in rejecting both my own thoughts and other people's after working them through and I've still felt they're wrong. Heifer story might still be right, however, but not in this scene.

The death scene is no better for seeing it a second time. In fact its deficiencies are all the more obvious, despite Rob's positioning and repositioning of the actors. The idea is that Granma lies dying in the Wilsons' tent, a sheet of tarpaulin on the floor upstage left, and after her death is lifted in the sheet to the grave upstage centre, where the tarpaulin is bunched around her, so masking her from the audience. During a later lighting change, Dorothy will quickly exit, unobserved. A great deal of time spent practising the lifting and carrying.

Then the hymn. Which today, possibly because the actors have spent so much time checking props, discussing tarpaulins, and generally arranging and re-arranging themselves, is sung with all the gusto of a glee club at a command performance. The hymn itself comes as a surprise to Duncan, as this is the first time he's been at rehearsals and I have not told him about it, wanting to see his immediate reaction. Glance sideways. His torso is thrust forward, elbows on knees, jaw set, eyebrows working like fast-moving knitting needles. The surprise has clearly not made his morning.

Although Peter Spears didn't look at all unsettled on Saturday, he does today. As if he's resisting the part. I wonder why? From conversations I've had with Rob, Albert, and some of the other actors, I have come to realise more than ever just what an important novel *The Grapes of Wrath* is to Americans. Or at least those Americans who read novels. It is not only a classic of their literature, it is a testament, a part of their history, inextricably woven into their national consciousness. Peter's caution might be something to do with the novel's iconographic enormity and with playing Tom Joad, whose previous creators so far have been Steinbeck himself and Henry Fonda in the film. And in America, the film is taught as much as the book. But it is apparent to me that Peter, if he has seen or studied the film, is an actor of far too much artistic honesty and integrity to want merely to duplicate something that has gone before, and is intent on creating his own Tom Joad.

He rehearses by choosing a strand he finds in the character and following it through every movement, every scene, to discover where it works and where it doesn't. Today, as on Saturday, he has chosen the introspective. Perhaps why he looks uneasy is that Tom's introspection comes in Act Two, not in Act One. In the Act One Tom and Casy scene, for instance, introspection appears as weakness, when he's talking to Ma in Scene Five ('You jus' gotta take ever' day as she comes'), as uncertainty, and in the gas-station scene when Tom threatens the attendant, as pathetic bumbling.

But Peter is a remarkably intelligent man, in his final year at Northwestern University in Chicago, and already has stage and film credits. Tall, good-looking in that clean-cut, fresh-faced American way, he seems naturally a quiet, studious sort of person. His Tom at the moment is coming primarily from that part of himself: reserved, actions determined by reason, a watchful, waiting kind of strength and solidity, but with a young, raw heart to it. He needs to let the rawness lead him more, let the reason come later under Casy's guidance. But what he is already experimenting with, and which is immensely interesting, is the capacity of Tom's intelligence; and Tom's intelligence, his innate senses and sensibility, is greater than his verbal expressiveness reveals. His may, in the end, be a controversial portrayal, but I am convinced already that it will be both compulsive and complex.

Noah still very camp.

What leapt out at me today is that there is nothing between Ma and Pa that persuades you they have been married for about thirty years. They stand monotonously apart from each other, talk at, instead of with, each other. That there is no relationship existing as yet is less worrying than the fact that there is not even the spark of one. In fact, the actors, Faith Geer and Albert, get on a lot better with each other off stage than they do as Ma and Pa onstage. If only some of the out-of-rehearsal trust they have in each other as professional acquaintances could be transferred into their work.

And Pa has become bullish – thrust-jawed and boggle-eyed.

Talked all this over with Rob. He takes careful notes, discusses points of his own. Then on to a talk on play-making in general in which, being both a playwright and a director, Rob is extremely pertinent and precise. The playwright knows what he has written, or believes he does. During rehearsals, directors, actors, and writers discover the piece afresh. And as I found my route with the play, so he must find his and the actors theirs. I should not be so impatient for progress yet. It takes time, and progress is being made.

Tuesday 21   The new Rose of Sharon–Connie sections finished, four of them. The first is for the Scene Three homecoming. When Tom first greets Rose of Sharon and Connie, I've expanded the dialogue to emphasise that Tom has not met Connie before, asking where he is from – Texas. Instead of Tom teasing Rose of Sharon that her baby will be born in a little white house with orange trees around the door in California, Connie now says the line, giving an indication of his ability to seduce Rose of Sharon and convince himself with dreams, something Tom makes a mental note of before being interrupted by Pa talking about Al.

Try to kill two birds with one stone by the next addition: integrate the heifer story and develop Connie. At the end of Scene Four, the family leave to begin packing up, with the exception of Tom and Al, who stay behind, Al to confirm that his brother really didn't break out of jail and to prove his sexual confidence by telling the heifer story.

Since Tom's imprisonment, the Joad family has lacked a mature second-in-command to Pa. Noah is too weak, Al too young. Connie has therefore not only joined the family but taken the place in it vacated by Tom, only to find it taken back from him when Tom unexpectedly returns and the family re-group around the prodigal. Clearly Pa relies almost exclusively on Tom, he is Ma's favourite, Al looks up to him, and Noah feels secure with him. Connie realises that he was only sitting in a chair that was always Tom's, and resents him for having to move out of it. Tom, meanwhile, is wary if not openly hostile to this stranger in their home. We need to see how the two men initially respond to each other and to the mutual aggression just below the surface, have a suggestion of their prowling around each other during the play, and how the knowledge of their distrust festers within Rose of Sharon.

Therefore, while Al is telling his story, Connie returns to find out what they're talking about. He interrupts their laughter, saying that it was quite an idea of Tom's to invite Casy along with them. (Earlier Connie objected, saying he 'wasn't family', before being silenced by Granma.) Tom replies that the family have known him a long time, implying that Casy is more a part of them than Connie is. Sure, says Connie, neither accepting nor rejecting. Look, says Tom, let me get this straight. You came all the way from Texas, met my sister, married her, and stayed. That's right, says Connie, met her at a dance. Tom – 'I met a few people from Texas. Never heard talk of people named Rivers.' Connie sees his opening – 'Guess you ain't. None of our family ever done time in jail.'

And he turns his back as Tom suddenly moves towards him, to be prevented by Al. The situation cools as fast as it flares, but the flame is lit and should be perceptible during the rest of the act in various ways. Connie, for example, will never support Tom or, in the incident at the gas station when he berates the attendant, be ready, as Al is, to fight alongside him.

The third addition is for Scene Six, after the dying Granma has been taken into the Wilsons' tent, and Ma asks Casy to pray for the old woman. The lights change to Connie and Rose of Sharon, a little apart from the others, stage right. The sequence brings out the chancer in Connie and Rose of Sharon's inability to discuss much more than the child she is carrying. Granma, says Rose of Sharon, looks bad. Connie only has eyes for the trucks still on the road, heading west. They could have travelled much further themselves tonight. Rose of Sharon demurs; they have to look after the eldest and weakest. Connie presses their own case: they must think of themselves. And (an afterthought) the baby of course. And did she not like the look of Oklahoma City when they passed through it earlier? Well, he could be like one of those guys they saw, wearing a light suit, eating in restaurants, earning big money. And they could buy things. An ice-maker. And stuff for the baby. Rose of Sharon – 'You're saying we should go back . . . leave the family . . .' Connie snaps that the family have made it pretty clear to him that he's not a Joad and besides, she should start thinking as a Rivers. I don't want to talk about it, she says.

It's a minor row which resolves itself by his concern for her following Granma's death. His leading the funeral hymn becomes a strategy of reconciliation.

This develops Rose of Sharon and Connie while adding the element of time to the death scene.

In Scene Eleven, I've re-written the love-making prelude, entirely changing its nature from one of harmony to separation. On the back of the truck, travelling across the desert at night, he touches her, caresses her. Tell me what it's going to be like when we get there, she says. And Connie begins to paint his pictures: owning a store, buying an ice-maker . . . But even if, says Rose of Sharon, even if you were just picking fruit and I was looking after the baby, we'd be happy, wouldn't we? Silence. Wouldn't we? You know, says Connie, turning away from her, you used to be just like a cat in bed. You've turned real serious.

In that moment of silence, Connie has seen reality: the months ahead of a whinging girl-wife and a squawking child while he scrabbles for miserable work, perpetually under the judgement of the Joads. In that moment he rejects her not only sexually but emotionally and intellectually. It is the moment he decides to leave and the moment Rose of Sharon fears he will.

Take the new passages tonight to Rob at the Linden Hotel where he's staying, just around the corner from the Royal Scots Club. Contretemps at desk with the rather dim, bleach-haired receptionist I discovered after a few minutes of bell-ringing, having a drink in the bar.

'Do you want to leave it, or what?' she asked, or rather accused, eyeing first the envelope suspiciously and then the bar door wistfully.

'Well, I'll give it to Mr Mulholland personally if he's in,' I said, expecting her to ring his room to find out.

Evidently concluding that here was an idiot treating the place like a hotel, and giving up on the bar and of finishing her drink within the next second at least, she stared at her nails with that special melancholia reserved for not particularly pretty girls for whom nails with flaking silver paint are a constant obsession.

She repeated what she'd said, I repeated what I'd said, twice, thinking I'd make more headway with the staff in the hotel's Thai restaurant (and why does a Georgian hotel in an Edinburgh backwater have a Thai restaurant?), several of whose heads were now stacked peering around the door like a Marx Brothers impression.

Approached topmost Thai head, explaining both to it and the girl that I wanted to leave the envelope and that it was very valuable, as a ploy to goad the girl into action and to have a backup should it prove necessary later. Eventually got the thing sorted out, girl crushing the envelope in two, ramming it into a pigeon-hole, and whizzing back into the bar.

Meet Paul Binotto on the way home. He talks seriously and enlighteningly about Connie. How would you sum him up, I ask, in a word? He's an adventurer, he says. Of course. That's it. That's what he is. He expands – Connie has probably been through this before, not to the extent of getting married, but that might have been forced upon him. Certainly he has hitched his wagon to a pretty girl before and will do again, although Rose of Sharon, in Sallisaw, was undoubtedly the love of his life. He did marry her. He did try to settle. He wants the audience to understand this, so they do not reject Connie out of hand. It's an important point. He leaves her when he does because he knows the present adventure is over. Where does he go after he runs out at Hooverville? Paul's theory is that he makes his way to Persky's peach ranch in Tulare County. But not for too long. There'll be another girl, another adventure. There always is for the Connies of this world.

There's a lesson here: always ask the actor.

And Paul Binotto is a very interesting actor. He has done several Broadway musicals: *Candide, Dreamgirls*; played Tobias Ragg in Sondheim's *Sweeney Todd* at New York City Opera, directed by Harold Prince in 1984; Shakespeare and off-Broadway shows. He is preparing an adaptation of Ovid's *The Love Cycle*, which he hopes to present off-Broadway in the fall, and left the Broadway cast of *Starlight Express* to play Connie and Paul Granger in *Hot l Baltimore*. He is very sharp and brings a keen and vivid intelligence to rehearsals.

Wednesday 22 Every day, rehearsals begin with a 'physicalisation' session led by Jodi. Apart from being the assistant director, she is also a mime artist and will be appearing with her own company, Mime Resources International, New York, on the Fringe.

Physicalisation sessions sound far more important and mysterious than they really are, being dressed up in the elaboration of the modern American language. In this country, they would be called warm-ups. They are vitally important, as no actor can work from a standing start, so to speak, in a rehearsal room as arctic as ours. However, with customary American thoroughness, they are taken to exhaustive lengths.

The actors touch toes, stretch, swing their arms, shout, walk the room in a circle as though taking shambling exercise in a prison yard, empathising to Jodi's instructions. 'C'mon, feel the heat . . . ' (Heads loll, eyes tighten). 'Very hot now . . . ' (Pace slows even more) 'Real dusty, you can't see . . . ' (An almost blind trudge) 'Hands feel gritty all the time . . . teeth, too . . . C'*mon*! Think about the last time you tried to get money out the bank . . . ' (This produces genuine looks of anguish) 'Ok . . . Come together.'

This is the signal for the group meditation process. 'Hold on to each other.' Everyone bunches together, their arms around each other's shoulders and waists, in a solid standing knot. 'Close your eyes . . . ' says Jodi, in a hypnotic hush. She pads around them, kneading a shoulder here, gently massaging kidneys there, pausing to hug one half of the scrum, then the other, clinging like a koala bear to a tree trunk. 'Get a sense of who you are . . .' Stepping back. 'Break when you feel you want to . . .'

After a few seconds the cluster disassembles, dazed-looking actors stumbling a few paces backwards, opening their eyes, coming to by flapping their arms, shaking their heads. Albert in particular, today, takes a full ten seconds to come round. Perhaps he should do this last thing at night. His insomnia could be over.

Have a look at a couple of pieces from Act One before moving on to the blocking of Act Two. Tom and Casy meeting scene. George has got rid of the harangue and the hang-loose, but their place has been taken by a type of King's Cross wino, a leering, rolling figure, breathy, slurring. The few lines of the song he sings at the opening of the scene ('Jesus is my Saviour', to the tune of 'Yes Sir, That's My Baby') are blurred and broken, an unaccountable silence between the 'Je' and the 'zuz', that sound as if they come from the bottom of a large bottle. Tom actually offering him a drink looks downright irresponsible and Casy actually chucking the bottle back completes the image of a ghoulishly maudlin Saturday night. He's staggering and so is the effect. Where on earth has it come from?

Temple Williams, like Peter at Northwestern University, has a good grasp of Al. Everything he does is very precise without being mannered. He is refining day by day, like a mason chipping away at a piece of stone.

David Beggs, playing a variety of smaller parts, Used-Car Salesman, Gas-Station Attendant, and Floyd Knowles among them, is producing some strikingly contrasted character portrayals, each one genuine and without a shadow of caricature. His Floyd Knowles today is very impressive for so early in Act Two rehearsals. Deliberate, straightforward, entirely without sentiment or begging pity.

Damien Kavanagh's Noah has now lost the campness and beginning to emerge as an interesting counterpoint to Tom and Al. He's also attached himself more to Pa, often standing only a few paces behind him, so the guilt Pa feels over his birth, when he gripped the skull and harmed the child, should begin to surface a little. Damien's Persky is too strident at the moment, but the cynical amiability of the politician isn't too far away.

Peter is still chasing the introspective in Tom, finding more use for it in Act Two, and therefore looking happier.

More stage furniture arrives today, and accommodating this into the blocking tends to slow things up.

Thursday 23   Rob is so far keeping to what he calls his 'time frame' for rehearsals, although blocking and running Act Two is proving tougher than Act One. This may be because the actors are, in a sense, going back to the beginning again and tackling something for the first time, although I would have thought that the experience of having worked Act One would have made the initial Act Two process easier instead of more difficult. It may be because (as I think) the weaker sections of the play are in this Act. It may be because I, at any rate, am realising that this is going to be a big lighting show, by which I mean that many of the transitions in time and place are signified by lighting changes, and as we won't be running with lights until we are in the theatre late in week four, it is difficult to gauge rhythm precisely, if at all. It may be that now, on the tenth day of a twenty-four-day rehearsal schedule, some of the company are beginning to feel the pressure of time. I know I am.

ED CAR SALESMAN: Good used cars! Cheap transportation, take ya all the way to California! Come right on in there, take a good look aroun'. We got Buicks, Nashes, DeSotos, Plymouths, Stars ... Take ya all the way to California!

CASY: Well, I figgered: 'Wh[y] got to hand it all on to Jesus[?] Maybe it's all men an' all w[e] we're s'posed to love. Mayb[e] what the Holy Sperit is: the [] sperit, the whole shebang. [Maybe] it's that ever'body's part of [one] soul.' All of a sudden, I kne[w] down it was true, an' I still k[now it].

TOM: You sure can't hol' no [job] with idears like that.

AL: Did ya bust out?

TOM: No. Done my time …

... Oh, I g-g-ue————— mighty near to goin' without you. An' I was

PA: This here la
goin' under the

E: We could be gettin' on
than this. You an' me
hink of ourselves…

A: We got to figger what to do. They's laws, they's always laws. You gotta report a
eath, an' when you do that, they take forty dollars for the undertaker, or jus' bury
her as a pauper. An' we never did have no paupers.

TOM: Maybe we got to learn. We never been booted off no lan' before, either.

CASY: In flight across th[e]
Panhandle ... In the da[rk]
migrant people scuttle [in the]
night, cluster like bugs [near]
light an' water. They wa[s]
flyin' from the same thi[ng,]
worry an' defeat...

PA: Last night we come to a camp. Got shade, an' water in pipes. Whole lotta
families stayin' there. Fat guy on the gate chargin' half-dollar apiece to stay, but
ever'body so wore out an' mis'ble, we jus' paid up. Seems like it costs now
jus' to lie under a tree...

Rob, however, is not. Not visibly. He seems impervious to stress, something that might be invaluable later on.

He is highly methodical and organised. He always has been and certainly is now. He sits each day in the rehearsal room on a high-backed chair, table pulled in to his waist, script beside spiral-bound A4 pad open at a clean page, pencils sharpened, erasers primed, a pack of mints or chewing gum to the ready. He commands simply by being there.

Roles are delegated: Jodi leads warm-ups, moves stage furniture, calls actors. Graham cues lines, does a hundred other things.

Rob watches, the pad filling with notes. Occasionally, he'll lope into the acting area, move an actor here or there with a quiet word, retreat, and watch from a corner to see a different perspective or, when taking only two or three actors through a few lines of a scene, hover at their shoulders. Mostly, though, he watches from the chair, the pencil seldom leaving his hand. Always, when I have been there, his voice is soft, conversational, the authority of a very good newsreader. I've a feeling he keeps a lot of what he's thinking to himself, but I may be wrong. Certainly he's very open with what he thinks should or should not be happening with the play when talking with me, is always available to discuss it, taking time to explain and deliberate, so I assume he's the same with the actors when I'm not there. But there is a certain impenetrability to Rob. Or perhaps not. Perhaps it's just that the actors talk so freely about themselves, about everything.

At the end of rehearsal each day, Rob gives notes. They are lengthy and detailed. Assiduous note-giving and meticulous note-taking is another indication of the extraordinary application and discipline of this company. They all have pads and pens with them and everything that Rob says is written down, after which the actors ask questions about the notes they have been given and raise issues and ideas of their own. Nobody begrudges anyone else time. It might be 11 o'clock at night, but nobody shows any sign of wanting to do anything else after a long day's rehearsal (some of them on other shows besides *The Grapes of Wrath*) than discuss the play and their work. Ideas are chivvied, dissected. Meanings turned over, movements analysed. A seminar atmosphere emerges in this draughty church hall, and in these sessions a lot of creative work is done. I know I've got a lot of ideas from being at them.

Listen to the actors, that's the thing.

Friday 24   Act Two is hellish. There seems so much wrong. Wrong with the script, that is, which makes the blocking look awkward and the pace dawdle almost to extinction.

Four major areas, two staging, two script. First, the dance sequence, particularly the Rose of Sharon–Old Woman sequence. Chris Ann is absolutely at sea in this and I don't blame her. She is a good actress, has several credits in Chicago theatres and is beginning to do interesting work with her character, but actresses rely on their scripts and this script in this scene is giving her nothing at all. Yet. Dorothy Bernard's Old Woman, like her initial Granma, has the words all right but not their place or sequence. The effect is one of incoherent battiness when it should be darkly disturbing.

Second: Casy's death. This is mimed – in slow motion. I myself am not clear as to how this should be staged, but it's certainly not in slow motion and (I've heard a rumour about this) a red light washing the stage.

Third: the bank-building the men do while Rose of Sharon is in labour, in an ill-fated attempt to stop the river flooding the boxcar. It has to be done off stage, at the most an impression of people running, creating a sort of arena wall behind Rose of Sharon, who is the focus of the scene. At the moment there's a lot of heavy footsteps and piling of trunks and boxes stage right . . .

Fourth: Al and Aggie. Well, I knew about that.

Have another look tomorrow, when the whole play is run for the first time, and when Duncan will be there to see it.

Saturday 25   Twelfth day of rehearsals, the day of the Great Talc Incident. Arrived at the church hall after dinner break at 7 p.m. for the first run-through of the entire play that, because of stops, re-starts, line calls, blocking problems and prop chaos, lasted over a third longer than it should have done, at almost three-and-a-half hours.

Alarmingly, both Chris Ann and Faith appear to have developed explosive chest colds. The run, actually a stumble, proceeded fitfully until the funeral scene, when it flopped into standstill, Chris Ann and Faith coughing like churning concrete mixers, purple-faced and swimming eyes, gulping water from a litre-size plastic Coca-Cola bottle.

This has obviously been a problem all day, judging from the way the rest of the cast silently look on as, at each volcanic eruption, Jodi patters forward with the water like a bashful mother hen.

In the break between Acts, asked Graham what was up. Apparently, it's the result of an earlier 'physicalisation' session when, in order for the cast to experience heat, Jodi had them lie on the floor while she intoned something about the effects of direct sunlight, and then, to simulate a duststorm, had liberally sprayed talc above them, clogging the air, and presumably their lungs, with powder. It explained the present hiatus. And the faint antiseptic smell.

Rob tends to take a back seat in these sessions, often absenting himself altogether, returning a minute before the actual rehearsal to take his seat behind his table, smooth his notepad, murmur a few words like 'Take a couple of seconds to believe who you are', and stipulate that all line calls should be spoken in character, something rarely, if ever, done.

I don't know whether he approves of these improvisation sessions or not. The actors seem to find them useful, though. First of all, they reinforce group awareness and therefore security, which Americans are very keen on. Secondly, they probably give the less-experienced actors a feeling of equality in the piece with the more experienced, which is essential in any theatrical endeavour, especially an ensemble. In fact, because of their psychological value and even, possibly, their apparent loopiness, they probably contribute more than the actual rehearsal itself to a feeling of corporate unity.

But at the same time I can't help feeling that this method-school-influenced emphasis on building environment and role through empathy (there's talk of some of the actors eating a meal, not as themselves but as the Joads) leaves the actors somewhat short-changed, technically, intellectually, and emotionally. It is as if, by this process, they expect to 'feel', to 'be', and sometimes I suspect that like Morales in *A Chorus Line*, that ghastly, manipulative musical, they feel nothing. Except a pain in the chest.

Perhaps some good emerges, perhaps not. But it does restrict them to a naturalistic approach and this play is not wholly naturalistic. The Joads themselves are not only the Joads but also representative of their type, and the play also requires certain characters – Casy and Tom most specifically, Ma and Pa to a lesser extent – to withdraw from their characters into narration, and therefore glide between naturalistic and non-naturalistic conventions.

Certainly, on the evidence of tonight's run, 'physicalisation' has not resulted in Ma and Pa beginning to look and sound like a couple married for thirty years, who have stoically scraped a living off the land and seen both erode; in Ma looking as though she has borne those four children; in Pa looking as though he is carrying a weight of loss, of hope, and then defeat. Neither is there any arc of growth and strength in Ma or disintegration in Pa, nor any sense of precisely where the crossover of ascent and descent happen in the play. Even allowing for the fact that Faith is still working script in hand and Albert has his pretty close by, the impetus is sluggish and monotonous.

The difficulties in Ma and Pa's scenes are emphasised because others, principally Noah, Al, Connie, and Rose of Sharon, are each word perfect and beginning, where possible, to evolve performances. In the case of Connie and Rose of Sharon, and Al in the section where he meets Aggie Wainwright, they are performances desperately in need of support by more and stronger lines to provide more accessible psycho-logical motivation and direction. Which is my problem. And although with work from me, those characters can be built to what they should be, I'm loath to pile more work on to Ma and Pa by altering their cue lines just as they are on the verge of actually remembering them.

Two other big problem areas. Props. The convention is that the stage is open, almost bare, such props as there are, a table, a few boxes, tarpaulins, flexible, kept to a minimum, used sparingly. They actually decrease in number during Act Two as the Act is leaner and the Joads have lost much of what they brought with them, either having dumped it or sold it along Highway 66, or left it during the burning of Hooverville Camp at the beginning of the act.

Yet tonight, in the scene following Hooverville, outside the Joad tent at the Government Camp at Weedpatch, Pa strides on having had a shave at the sanitation block – a facility the Joads are in awe at and which, to their wonder, has flushing toilets and hot water – carrying a large pink por-celain washing bowl, an item I have never seen in rehearsals before now, and plonks it down on the large table we used as the truck in Act One.

Furthermore, Ma delivered her line 'Ya had a shave', almost ten feet away from him. The point is that this scene is light, quietly humorous, has a feeling of tranquility after the burning and provides an interlude after the previous hardships and before those to come. As much for the audience as for anyone else. But this has to be established in such lines between Ma and Pa. I always imagined her touching his face, their putting their arms around each other.

Second: the following dance sequence, as I always suspected, is a disaster. My disaster. Badly written and, in my view, the weakest section of the play, but for the moment I can't work out precisely why. As it stands, Ma and Pa's impromptu steps on hearing from Al there is to be a dance on the Saturday night, is a choreographed square dance rather than unexpected boisterousness, after which Ma and Pa freeze in mid-bow, held while Mrs Thomas tells Tom of the cops' decision to raid the camp. The scene following Tom and Al's decision to keep a lookout, the Old Woman accosting Rose, is played at crematorium pace and doesn't even look like succeeding in doing what it is supposed to: to induce such fear in Rose that she might lose her child, that it is another spur to her eventual betrayal of Tom. And, again, that's my problem. And, again, as for a remedy, tonight, I'm lost.

Later a post-mortem with Rob. Tackle him on washbowl.

'Ah, that won't be there in performance,' he says.

'But why in rehearsal, then?'

'It's something actors need. They like to work with things before they work without them. We'll lose it soon enough.'

As to the large table, it emerges that Rob sees it as a table, whereas Duncan and I and, more cogently, the designer, see it as a table only in Sallisaw at the top of Act One, where it symbolises home and domesticity; thereafter it becomes, turned upside down, the truck; and in Act Two is almost off stage until lit as part of a boxcar or a section of the barn interior at the very end of the play.

This is an example of our infrequent, but significant, cross-currents of thought, where our thinking about the play is not clear between Rob and ourselves, because we've assumed on odd details that each party knows what the other is thinking. So we're diverging and foundering when we should be converging, honing, refining.

It is depressing at this stage to feel so adrift, yet Rob is placatory, in control.

Sunday 26   On reflection, what I saw last night as dismally time-consuming and fogged, the 'physicalisation', the filling of the play with extraneous bits and pieces, the text and embryonic performances blurred by a gestural, plodding, and unfocused rehearsal, is, in reality, only the company approaching their part of the work in the same manner as I approached mine nine months ago. You build in order to reduce, you assemble everything you think you might want to find out what you actually need. The script was massively long and wandering until it evolved, over time, into its present form. Which will not be the final one.

That's rational. But no less worrying.

In pouring rain Duncan and I take his dog for a walk in the park. We do about three-and-a-half laps, dog does about six. Duncan saw the run-through with me last night. Both agree, show in a ghastly state.

On we trudge. Rain drips through trees.

Silence.

Connie and Rose of Sharon very good, he says, very explorative.

And Al, too, I say.

Yes, Al, too.

Tom getting there.

Definitely. Definitely Tom getting there.

Nothing can disguise the fact, though, that half-way through rehearsals, we have slipped back so far that what we have now is a corpse. A collection of inert little bits interspersed by other little bits, their apparent liveliness only a virtue of their not being quite as inert as the rest.

Rain seeps through my shoes and socks. There we stand, dog hurtling about, presiding over a corpse. Or stillbirth, whichever way you choose to look at it. The thing to do is phone Rob. Speak out. Get something moving.

Two hours later, having phoned, we flap wetly round to the Royal Scots Club. Janet Scarfe, the designer, is fitting soundproofing and white sheeting to the underneath of the rostrum in the cavernous basement room. Lengths of scaffolding lie on the floor. A theatre is taking shape.

Into a side room with Rob. A large, dusty room, badly carpeted, filled with a jumble of chipped and scratched chairs, and red Formica-topped tables that look as though they were taken from a skip outside a closed-down café. Regimental prints hang on nicotine-stained walls. In the wintry light of a summer afternoon, rain battering on the windows, faces fading into shadow, we begin.

Rob's first in. Could we cut the fry-potatoes Ma takes to Tom in the culvert scene?

'What's wrong with the fry-potatoes?'

'The actors are given them every day for their lunch upstairs, there's no choice and now everyone's fed up with fry-potatoes; it's a thing with them.'

So we cut the fry-potatoes.

I launch in on the Joads not looking like a family. I don't know why they don't, they just, exasperatingly, don't.

Yes, he knows this.

And as yet there is no dramatic line to Faith Geer's Ma, not even a suggestion of one, no sense of the point at which her natural strength as a woman, as Ma Joad, as an American matriarch, begins to become the dominating force of the family. In my view, and Duncan's, this turning-point is the moment in Act One, Scene Eight, when she first defies Pa, picks up the jack-handle from the truck and threatens him with it. It is an extremely important action, central to the play. It is the crucial change of gear for this woman who at the end of the play stands like a pillar of resilience, and from whom the rest of the family, in whatever measure, derive their guidance and sustenance. And right now, all that's emerging is a sweet, apple-cheeked Mom with a quirky temper.

Ah, says Rob, but is this scene in fact a, or the, turning-point? We see her strength earlier on, don't we, in Scene Four, for example, when she insists that Casy comes with them, and when she tells Pa in no uncertain terms that no Joad has ever refused a man food and shelter? The power of her will is quite evident before Scene Eight.

Search through the script to identify at which point authority can be said to transfer decisively from Pa to Ma. After labyrinthine um-ing and ah-ing in the advancing gloom, decide, not surprisingly, it's when she picks up the jack-handle. Decide, furthermore, that the actual speech as it stands is fine.

Is it then Pa's response that diffuses it from one of explosive tension to something sounding more like a minor squabble over which vegetable to have for dinner? Pa's response to Ma's aggression is, 'Jesus, I never seen her so sassy'. It's from the novel. But Pa, instead of being alarmed, is highly amused, last night actually turning his back on Ma to share the joke with the boys.

The problem could be, says Rob, the change in the meaning of the word 'sassy' from the 1930s to the present day. In the Steinbeckian, old sense it meant belligerent, nowadays it means streetwise, chic, hip, something of course Ma is not. And Albert is perhaps using the word in its current meaning and having great and understandable difficulty in making it ring true in that situation.

This explains, or could explain, a lot. We change Pa's response to 'We made up our min' to go', and then Ma: 'No. You jus' made up *your* min' '. It sharpens the confrontation and should help the actors. But the core of the problem is still getting Faith to the point where Ma's speech works.

Move on to the Act Two bank building. I explain breaking-of-waters themes, etc., in the stillbirth–flood sequences.

Yes, says Rob, exactly the way I see it. But do we actually want to see the building of the bank on stage?

No.

Fine. Neither does he.

On the rather delicate but nonetheless vital issue of why, if the three of us don't want to see half the cast piling up trunks and pushing them over, are we actually seeing just that, Rob says the actors are 'working through' it.

The actors, therefore, are 'working through' the lobbing of the liquor bottle, the bringing on of the pink porcelain washbowl, and the stacking of the trunks, in order to be deprived of doing all of them.

Silence.

We work slowly on down the ledger, the most important details are Ma and Pa, and Casy the wino, Casy snorting and heaving and moaning and singing about God and life. Rob is irked at the direction in which George has gone and is determined to snap him out of it. He remains convinced, however, as do I, of not only a significant performance, but that he'll lead the reviews.

But the central, unavoidable problem is Ma and Pa. We keep coming back to it. They underpin the entire structure of the play – if they fall, the play falls. Though Rob adds that Albert is a late developer as an actor.

'Don't worry. He'll put it all together in the last few days. It's his way.' He also points out, answering an unasked question, but I suspect one he is astute enough to gather that we are searching for the appropriate words for, that during extensive auditions for Pa, Albert was the actor who consistently gave the most interesting reading. He has the part on merit, and not because of his AFT staff position. And having seen a Press photograph of Faith and Albert as Ma and Pa, I agree they look remarkable. It is extraordinarily evocative. Both look like workers on the land. Faith stares into the camera, strong, defiant, and somewhat distrusting; Albert stands just behind her left shoulder, weary, surly, and suspicious. If they can achieve and sustain a performance equal to that picture, they'll be on course. But can they?

Monday 27   Thirteenth day of rehearsals. Didn't go up to the church hall today as Rob is working on short sections from Act Two and there is little I can add for the moment.

He does report, though, that the Rose of Sharon and Connie additions for Act One work well.

Duncan rings to say that a chap from *The List*, an Edinburgh and Glasgow sub-version of *Time Out*, is to interview us on the production. Scheduled for Wednesday at the Royal Scots Club.

Tuesday 28   The lowest point yet. Today, the Ma and Pa problem narrowed itself down specifically to Ma, flamed into crisis, exploded and, no doubt on the principle that one grenade never made an attack nor one firework a display, lit and fired several others for good measure. Today began with me peacefully sorting my notes prior to writing a revised Al and Aggie sequence, untouched since the read-through. Today ended with my feeling a potent mix of despair and resentment.

6.30 p.m. Phone call from Rob. He's at his hotel, devoting an evening to working on the lighting design. The voice is even enough but its tautness reveals he's rattled about something. And if Rob is rattled, it means something's up. He reports that rehearsals yesterday were bad, today worse, much worse, execrable, the most unproductive so far. Unproductive to the extent of there not actually being a rehearsal in the real sense of the word because Faith forgets most of her lines, and when she does remember them cannot co-ordinate the blocking with them.

This is doubly dismaying news: first, about Faith herself, but second, that by this time the cast should have left the script behind and be concentrating solely on performance. Faith's anxiety and stops and starts are, according to Rob, beginning to affect the other actors and tempers are beginning to simmer, which is having a kind of boomerang effect on Faith, unnerving her into forgetting even more lines. Chris Ann is becoming especially exasperated because much of Rose of Sharon's Act Two dialogue is with Ma, and Faith's helplessness is consistently throwing her concentration.

Rob: 'Act Two is running well when I can get them to do it, but I haven't been able to run Act One since Saturday, and that's not good. I'm really concerned about it. Not panicking yet, but certainly not pleased. I was very put out today because Faith could really blow it. I was put out and I showed it. It could be a watershed.'

Well, maybe the quiet, cautious Rob getting tough is what the show needs.

Faith and Albert are closeted away somewhere with Jodi right now, banging relentlessly through the lines, tonight and tomorrow and for as long as it takes. And tomorrow's run-through of the play has been postponed until Thursday. And I get the impression I'm being prepared for a hobble instead of a run.

I feel unsettled partly because there is little I can do. I'm going to resist – if I'm asked, and I don't think Rob would – cutting or changing lines that are right purely because an actor can't remember them. After all, Ma is one of the parts, on the page at least, that's given us – Rob, Albert, Duncan, myself – the fewest problems. But should I cut if parts of speeches are perpetually dropped, cues for other actors fluffed, and words changed, sometimes ludicrously? An example – in Act One, Scene Seven, in the line, 'Pa was sayin' you can' cross the border, you bein' on parole,' the word 'parole' more often than not comes out as 'patrol'. But I can't change it. There's no substitute.

Duncan knocks on the door halfway through all this and afterwards I bring him up to date. He's not enamoured. He's terse, in fact. Especially as today he rang the Fringe advance box office and found we've sold seventy tickets for the play already, which, two weeks before opening, is considered a very good number. The normal advance at this stage is, apparently, fifteen, and you shouldn't be too bothered if you've sold none at all. By this time last year, *Playing For Time*, the Arthur Miller première that won AFT a Fringe First award, had an advance of about thirty. Knowing there's ticket holders out there somewhere makes Rob's news even more disturbing. Duncan disappears home, muttering.

I speculate whether we're at the stage of having to find another Ma and, if not, how long it might be before that decision has to be taken, and how it would affect the company . . . Could we find another Ma and still open in a week and a half? Can we open in a week and a half as it is? I wonder what the problem is with Faith. Some kind of psychological block, must be, though what, I don't know. Or. The hard fact. She just cannot remember her lines. She is in her mid-sixties and that calibre of retentiveness has gone. It happens.

But Rob has seen her on stage often, knows her work well. She is working quite extensively at home, has two films due for release soon . . . I don't know.

Minutes later, Duncan is on the phone. Terseness has wound up a few notches, like the turn of a key on thumbscrews, into extreme pithiness. He reminds me that Rob aimed to have the show run-ready by this Saturday. As next Wednesday, Thursday, and Friday are timetabled for technical rehearsals in the theatre, as little basic character development work as possible should be left to week four. This Saturday's schedule Duncan sees as having gone by the board. But his real point, a tangent from the Faith emergency, is that it transpires that Rob has only telephoned me (so far), and despite the fact that I assured Rob that I would pass the news on to Duncan as he was there, Duncan neverthe-less sees his lack of a personal telephone call, and that Rob did not request that the three of us meet, as another contravention of our tripartite discussion agreement, and is phoning to tell me that he is about to phone Rob and tell him so.

I think it's over-reacting as well as probably being the last thing Rob needs, but Duncan is insistent.

9 p.m. Phone call from Rob. The voice is now distinctly embattled. Apparently Duncan, rather than phoning, shot up the road to the Royal Scots Club in search of Rob, but came across Hal instead. This gets complicated, but it appears that Duncan alleged to Hal that Rob had acted unconstitutionally, as he put it (or as someone has put it), and that somewhere along the line had emerged the accusation that I had been asked by Rob not to relay an account of his phone call to me, to Duncan. Rob is now calling me in an attempt to discover how the latter misunderstanding might have occurred, something I really don't have an idea about, but more pertinently to point out that he has more than enough problems of his own with actors, mapping out lighting cues, and tracking down sound tapes that have so far failed to arrive from New York, without getting into unnecessary personal confrontations. Do I know where Duncan is now? He'd rung his flat but Janet reported him out, tried his office but no answer. I say between rapidly gritting teeth that I don't, but suspect I will before the night is much older.

Abandon Al and Aggie doing nothing much in their migrant camp by the cotton fields and insulate myself beneath headphones and Mahler's 'Resurrection Symphony'. Soothing and, at the end, gloriously uplifting and inspiring. Not that it has much time to soothe or inspire as . . .

10 p.m. Phone rings. Duncan again. Fuming. Hardly able to speak, actually. Just the odd word punctures aggressive silence. He'd just phoned Rob. Possibly from home, though he didn't say. But assume it was because that is where he is now. He'd charged Rob with ignoring agreements, etc. Rob had countered by accusing him of throwing a tantrum and Duncan had denied this. Furiously. To which Rob had said that if the conversation continued in the present atmosphere, he would hang up on him. Which Duncan challenged him to do. Which Rob then did.

Long pauses throughout all this, which I attempt to fill, not particu-larly comprehensively, with 'Yes . . . , I see . . . ' More than once it is only the absence of the dialling tone that indicates he has not hung up on me. More than once, my own increasing agitation and despondency makes me wish I could hang up on him.

Perhaps Rob should have called the three of us together, or I should have suggested it. But it would have achieved nothing. And the issue of whether he or I did or did not (if that is the issue) is of no relative importance whatsoever, and has only succeeded in swamping the real crisis of Faith and the future of the play, which, after its initial appearance, hasn't raised its head above the increasingly hostile claims and counter-claims. And absolutely nothing, in my view, is as important as the play.

Suddenly realise I'm still standing here, hanging on, as we embark on a tense cross-examination.

Was I going to the run on Thursday?

Yes, of course. Wasn't he?

No.

Ah.

(Short silence.)

Was he going to the interview tomorrow?

No. For reasons I know about.

(What on earth are they? Desperately uncomfortable silence.)

Because you don't enjoy interviews?

No. On his own he can handle interviews, no problem. But with three other people there . . .

Well, you go instead of me.

No. I should go.

(This is maddening. I'm almost crushing the telephone receiver. Then, from his end:)

'But I want to know every script change, everything that happens.'

This is really extraordinarily difficult. Conversation jolts into nothing. We sign off with no plans for getting in touch, tomorrow or any other day.

Hardly a moment before the phone rings again. Snatch up the receiver. Rob. Told him Duncan had just phoned. Told him I now have very little idea of whatever it is we are supposed to be discussing. Was I seeing Duncan tomorrow? Not that I know of. Decide to let things rest. Ring off amicably enough.

I am depressed, angry, and feel an unfocused resentment that this has happened. But looked at logically, or as logically as I can look at it in this mood at 1 o'clock in the morning, we are obviously each under stress and probably none of us realised the extent of it until the Faith crisis caused it to erupt. Rob probably feels besieged. I certainly feel powerless. Duncan possibly feels the same as well as realising, perhaps for the first time, perhaps not, that the play could be a failure.

Yes, of course it could.

Wednesday 29   Fifteenth day of rehearsals. Work mostly on short sections, including the transition from the boxcar to the barn. Cut a few words out of this, not because of the actors' having any difficulty but to speed things up a little.

Miranda McGrath seems to be enjoying her role as the Barn Girl. Her acting is too forced and laboured at present, but once she relaxes and finds her own pace, she'll improve.

Later, the interview at the Royal Scots Club with the chap from *The List*. Rob, Albert, Paul Binotto, and myself. The chap walks in the room fifteen minutes late and with no apology, but as Rob had gone looking for him and found him lurking in some other part of the building, he might have arrived there on time and the apology, if any, proffered only to Rob. Chap kicks off by announcing that he doesn't intend to write very much about the production, very little in fact, as they intend to preview as many as they can. That's fine, but the almost gloating manner in which he says this implies that we should count ourselves pretty lucky to be included in the first place. Or is this non-apology and inference business the beating little wings of last night?

What a vacuous question 'What was the challenge of . . . ' (in this case, *The Grapes of Wrath*) is. It's not a question at all, more of a buffer against which the unprepared interviewer can pin the interviewee and wait while he (the interviewee) flounders about feeling embarrassed trying to extract some strand out of the work he has done that might interest the blank face in front of him. Seasoned interviewees always have some stock answer to bring out for dud questions, but I'm not a seasoned interviewee. I improvise something about the novel being a classic and why, at which the chap looks highly sceptical. He then asks me something about adapting *The Grapes of Wrath* from a Scottish perspective, something it had never occurred to me to do, had not done, and would not do . . .

Rob is bowled some bland stuff about the company . . .

Still, I suppose we glided over the ground, viewed it, or part of it from some way off. Hit some of the bases, as Rob would say. Did say, I think.

The chap had plonked an ageing pocket tape-recorder in the centre of the table, three feet or more away from us all, the sort of thing that usually plays back a kind of oscillating hiss more than anything else, so everything we said will probably be inaudible. However, he did take a few scratchy notes, so I expect something will result.

Thursday 30   A momentous day. Arrive at the rehearsal room at 7.15 tonight as the cast are gathering after their dinner break for the postponed run-through. A few minutes later, in comes Duncan, Rob not far behind, difficulties clearly having been resolved.

On top of this, an excellent run. Something, perhaps Rob's 'watershed', certainly his determination, perhaps Jodi slogging through the lines for hours with Faith and Albert, which appears to have paid off (Faith is much surer on the lines tonight than she has been before, but not completely in the clear yet), has brought a renewed sense of purpose to the play and a lightness of touch it hasn't had before. There's an ensemble spirit, the actors trust each other, are visibly more relaxed, are more certain of where they and the play are going. There's sustained eye contact for the first time, the family hug each other, Ma and Pa touch, Casy claps Tom on the shoulder.

That the sociological and personal dimensions of the play are beginning to focus is underlined by the addition of the sound cues that Rob has compiled and that we hear for the first time tonight, albeit only on a Walkman rigged up to two miniature speakers.

From the time the house doors open until the play begins, there is fifteen minutes of snatches of American popular songs of the 1930s, radio advertising jingles, and excerpts from comedy shows, linked by the static of a wireless being tuned and retuned. This fades as the house lights go down, and a low stage light picks out the cast grouped impassively together as the sound of a fierce, destructive wind quickly fades up, and then down as the tableau light itself fades. Another light comes up on Tom, who speaks his first 'Night after night in my bunk . . . ' speech in silence, before his light darkens and a third picks out Pa and the wind returns for his 'Ever' year we got a good crop comin' . . . ' speech.

It should work magnificently: the coy, tinkling jingles and the *Lone Ranger* theme set against a dark, inexorable rhythm of dim light and piercing, devastating wind.

The play's 'theme', used in some Act One scenes changes but more importantly during the road scenes when the truck is moving, is Woody Guthrie's 'Struggle Blues'. Raw, driving, train-time harmonica.

Immediately after Used-Car Salesman ends Scene One with 'Great used cars! Take ya all the way to California!'; Al Jolson's live recording of 'Yes Sir, That's My Baby', links into Scene Two and fades as Casy takes up the music with his own words and his own rhythm. Scene Four, the family huddle, is prefaced by a radio time-check, 'It's 8 p.m. B-U-L-O-V-A Bulova Watch Time'; Scene Seven, the gas-station scene, ends, ironically, with a radio advertisement for Esso, a bright male voice concluding with 'Happy Motoring'. Before the Joads set out from the Colorado River to cross the desert at the end of Scene Ten, they offer Wilson some pork scraps and a couple of dollars. He is too proud to take it, so they leave them on the ground. The last we see of Wilson is him gazing half gratefully, half resentfully after the disappearing Joads, then dropping to his knees and scrabbling up his gifts as 'Brother, Can You Spare a Dime?' plays.

There is much less recorded sound in Act Two, reflecting the Joads' increasingly bleak circumstances and that they are now absolutely out of reach of the world they once knew. In fact, the only tape sound is the gradual, and then tumultuous rain from the culvert scene onwards, and the keeling over of the tree during the flood. The rain eases during the barn sequence, then returns after Tom's final 'I'll be there' speech with a sudden vengeance. Just as suddenly it stops as the lights fade at the end of the play, Tom and Rose of Sharon looking out into the audience.

I remember *Three Men on A Horse* I saw at the beginning of the year. It is a similar device, but Rob has done a superb job with the sound here, thoroughly integrating a vital part of the play with its other themes. There is a far greater sense of the play's 'world', its historical and cultural context, and it has helped the actors enormously.

Peter Spears is broadening and defining Tom all the time. Tonight he brings forward the maturing of the character, the complexity of his internal struggle in channelling immediate and unfocused responses into reason and responsible action. He sets the turning-point of this process, when Tom begins to leave one part of himself behind and consciously emulates Casy, in the sequence in Scene Eight when he and Casy stay behind to fix the Wilsons' car. Casy asks Tom if he's noticed that at the makeshift roadside camps where they've stopped, a communal spirit, a code of behaviour forms as if by itself amongst strangers forced together by shared troubles.

No, says Tom.

Casy presses further. There's thousands of travellers, all heading west, running, like refugees after a war. Surely he's noticed that?

Look, says Tom, I'm just putting one foot in front of the other. I couldn't think of anything for four years in McAlester, in case I went mad. I thought it would be different when I came out. But it's the same thing.

Peter has taken this speech of Tom's in different ways: rejecting Casy, meeting him head-on, but now playing it as if doubting the solidity of his own thoughts, his own privacy, inviting Casy in some way to become his mentor. It's an interesting development.

George McGrath, after Rob's intervention, has dropped Casy the garrulous wino. He has taken something from it, however, a remnant of the glory-calling voice of Casy the preacher, something he had earlier but became lost in the bottle. But now it is far more controlled and used sparingly in the moments in Scene Two when Casy talks about his past, allowing us a glimpse, almost a flashback, of what Casy must have been like as an orator. But much more importantly, the lightness, the almost tongue-in-cheek way in which he uses the voice, tells us about his apparent rejection of his own past and former self. His response to Tom's initial recollection 'You're the preacher', is firm: 'I *was* the preacher', then jaunty, 'Reverend Jim Casy'. On this line he raises his arms; fleetingly, there is the sign of the cross. Simultaneously we see that he is empty handed, defenceless. Self-confessedly a preacher no longer, perhaps, but maybe still a preacher of a sort deep down inside. It is very perceptive, discreet, and truthful.

Later, when he is asked by Ma to pray for Granma, and Mrs Wilson to say a prayer for her, Casy's voice becomes quiet, almost fragile, as if he's trying to avoid the words in some way. Yet there is a strength of stillness and a presence in the man himself. It is fascinating to see how George is using these two strands of Casy's past and present, using one to inform and qualify the other. And what is also emerging is his attitude towards others. In the homecoming scene he moves away from the family and then edges closer, the same at the gas station, the same at Hooverville. When he needs to be, he is always just on the edge of our vision. Casy the observer. Exactly right.

It is extremely instructive to watch actors like Peter and George rehearsing.

There are a few other points: Duncan and I agree to cut the Act One, Scene Four heifer story. At long last. The Connie addition at the end of the scene makes it superfluous, it has always grated, and it is suddenly very noticeable to both of us that with Casy's haltered heifer–service quip following pretty closely, there's a hell of a lot of jokey cattle stuff in the first twenty minutes of the play.

The Act One hymn is working better. More ragged and no Mormon harmonies.

I still don't find a Mrs rather than a Mr Thomas in Act Two convincing. But perhaps it is more the fact that it is interspersed with the dance sequence, and those scenes are woefully deficient. Not because of Rob, not because of the actors, because of the script. And there's not so much time left for me to get it right. Or to write Al and Aggie. I've become so diverted by our feuds that I've done very little to Al and Aggie.

Hunt out Heather Hitt, the actress playing Aggie, and ask her Aggie's perceptions of Al. She is very intuitive and I take several notes to work up into something tomorrow.

Friday 31   The jack-handle scene solved. But it begins as still an immense problem. Ma has just threatened Pa. Tom's following line is 'Ma, what's eatin' you?' but the simmering, prowling rebellion is just not there in Ma's response. Rob runs the speech again and again, Faith trying it continuing her onslaught of anger, then very quiet, controlled, venomous. Neither comes off. Without warning, Rob jumps to his feet, strides quickly across to Faith, and bellows 'Ma, what's eatin' you?' inches from her nose. Rob has never done anything like this before, not that I've seen, anyway. Immediately tension is switched on like a light, immediately, after a momentary bewilderment, Faith draws herself up and bitterly but with great dignity lists exactly what it is that is eating Ma. What have they got left in the world? Nothing but the family. Their house was pushed down so they came out onto the road. Granma died. Rose of Sharon and Connie are secretly cooking up little plans of their own. And now Tom is saying the family should split up . . .

It is a revelatory moment. Suddenly the speech is charged with a new and vital emotion. Ma is angered, but its initial fire has become something much deeper. What she is doing is dredging up latent powers of resilience and determination and perhaps surprising herself in the process. She sees the Joads' plight in terms of a personal attack and in the force of her natural defences, Ma has discovered more about herself. It took this sudden rehearsal confrontation for Faith to find this in Ma, and for Peter to hit upon how to deliver Ma's cue.

They try it again. It works. On the surface, the speech is quiet, but it is full of iron, which it never had before, and consequently is subtle and effective.

Costume parade tonight at the Royal Scots Club, at which the actors try on their costumes for the first time. An exhausting affair held in a basement corridor crowded with fifteen actors, Rob, Hal, Duncan, and myself, and during which the corn-haired costume designer whose name, I have belatedly discovered, is Sue Ellen Rohrer, looks harassed and, at more than one point, despairing.

Working on costumes for five shows simultaneously on minimum budget, finding clothes by scouring second-hand shops, begging from private sources and Rep theatres, altering the passable to make it as exact as possible, and then have weeks of research, footwork and work pored over, criticised, and sometimes rejected out of hand in two hours, is a tough business.

But she must be used to it. Thrive on it. She has designed for over twenty-five productions, mostly in New York, and assisted on the costumes for *Cats* and *42nd Street* on Broadway.

I find it difficult to make any assessment of *The Grapes* costumes in this cramped and dim space where distance between each other is at the very most six feet, and only that achieved by shoving people into an adjacent corridor. Albert, though, looks terrific: dull dungarees over a shabby vest, buttoned down the front, old hat, boots. Duard Mosley's Wilson, in a rather tight black suit and clutching a narrow-brimmed black hat, looks, because Duard is tall and solidly built, unfortunately like Oliver Hardy standing next to Damien Kavanagh's shorter, slimmer Noah. Tom, in denims and wide-lapelled blazer jacket, is too much the college graduate but Casy, in grey cotton shirt and loose-fitting trousers, looks fine. Rose of Sharon, in a knee-length flower print dress, the shoulders rippling with ruffles, is too cute and reminds me of a Mabel Lucie Atwell cartoon. And Granma, in linen cap, shawl, and floor-length skirt, looks as though she's waiting for her entrance in a production of *The Crucible*.

Sue Ellen, pins radiating from between brilliant white teeth, is already working with scissors and making furious notes about changes and distressing (the process of quickly breaking down a fabric so that it looks old). The costume parade is really for her benefit than anyone else's. The first time she's actually seen the clothes worn by actors, it is her first chance to test and change her ideas.

AUGUST

Saturday 1   The first indications of the Festival.
The scaffolding for the Tattoo, great wings of steel webbing, rises up
from the Castle esplanade, and as I walk up to rehearsal tonight,
pantechnicons are parked outside the Assembly Rooms and red plastic
seating and scaffolding for lighting rigs are being unloaded.

Talk for a time to George McGrath. He's done twelve productions
for New York Shakespeare, including the recent Broadway revival of
The Threepenny Opera, and several plays with the director Richard
Foreman. He's worked for LaMama and at several other theatres; was
Antonio to Sigourney Weaver's Portia in the CSC Rep production of
The Merchant of Venice last year, and is soon to start work on a one-man
show written especially for him about one of Eugene O'Neill's sons,
1988 being the centenary of O'Neill's birth. Both watching and talking
to George is teaching me a great deal; a gentle, intuitive, and very
generous man.

Run-through: Rob: 'Hell or high water run. If you lose a line, cover, if
you really can't, ask for the line in character and Graham will give it to
you. Okay, places. Preset lights out. Blackout. Tableau lights up. Out.
Tom's light up . . . '

The first act runs fairly smoothly. Only one or two misfires on lines
and an odd bit of confusion over the peach-pickers-wanted-in-
California handbills on which the Joads and Wilsons are pinning their
hopes, and which they discuss when they meet. For some reason Ivy
Wilson did not produce his handbill from his pocket, leaving Pa unable
to produce his own to compare, and Wilson to pronounce it identical to
his own.

The second act is still uneven and crumbles towards the end. It has a
tired, run-down feel to it. Not waving but drowning, or not drowning but
waving? Difficult at almost midnight after a week like this has been, to
say.

Sunday 2   Spend the morning finishing the
new Al and Aggie piece. Cut my original completely, the eight lines in
which they plan marriage at the end of Act Two, Scene Ten, immediately before Rose of Sharon tells Ma in Scene Eleven that she has
betrayed Tom, and replace it with a longer section beginning with Al

telling Aggie the heifer story. (Yes, the heifer story again; but placing it shortly after Hooper's Ranch and before the build-up to the flood will, hopefully, give the despair something to play against.) Hearing the story, Aggie laughs. They relax with each other. It is evident from their conversation they have known each other some time. The scene develops as they compare their experiences of the road and look ahead to the possible difficulties facing them together. It shows the maturing of Al, gives an indication of events beyond the end of the play and their realism contrasts sharply with the Connie and Rose of Sharon story.

Duncan has come up with an alternative plan. He has Al and Aggie meeting for the first time when the Joads arrive at the boxcars at the beginning of Scene Ten and includes the heifer story there. He adds an extra few lines during Scene Ten, Al telling Ma that he is off to see Aggie, Ma commenting on his evident affection for her to Pa after he's gone. The later eight lines are preserved intact, and there are extra lines for Al near the end of Scene Eleven, before Ma, Pa, and Rose of Sharon leave for the barn. As the text stands, Al tells them that he and Aggie (who has been assisting Ma with Rose of Sharon) intend to stay together, and Ma gives them her blessing. Duncan proposes adding here information that actually precedes the stillbirth sequence in the novel: that he and Aggie want to be married and he plans to find a job in a garage.

This last idea is excellent. Previously, Al had drifted out of the picture somewhat; this gives him a stronger ending, almost equal in importance to Tom and Rose of Sharon. Each achieves, in his or her own way, a resolution.

But my objection to his other proposals is that they do not resolve the problem of the present scene – that it is so short, so incidental as to hardly register. Adding an extra fragment of even fewer lines will surely only emphasise the thinness of the Al and Aggie strand in the play.

His objection to my solution is that he is adamant that Al would not tell Aggie the heifer story, if indeed he tells it to her at all, in almost the same breath as he deliberates their future together. By that time, he is no longer a bit of a lad. And second, I am trying to pack too much information into too short a space.

We try – a mistake – to barter our way towards something on which we both agree. Cutting the heifer story is no great loss for either of us, except that it reduces Duncan's first episode to a mere glance from Al as Aggie flits across the stage, something neither of us are happy about. My determination to remove those appalling eight lines of mine, bound up with what I recognise as obduracy in wanting to preserve in some form my own replacement, leads us, after two hours of inconclusive rambling, to contemplating the absurd compromise of cutting Aggie out of the play altogether.

This is clearly untenable. It is unprofessional to write the part out of the play at this stage on such derelict reasoning, unforgivably cruel to the actress who has conscientiously attended rehearsals for four lines. It will injure cast morale, possibly irretrievably, and be detrimental to the play.

Off we go to the Royal Scots Club to put the situation to Rob. It occurs to me that this is the first time since the conflict over the Tom ending in March, that Duncan and I have been so diametrically opposed over the script. There have been differences of opinion, yes, several, but more or less amicable and never before have we had to call in a referee, a difficult position in which to place your director.

Rob's news is that the lighting operator who appeared for the first time at the run-through last night, will not now be working on this show. His grandfather has died and he will be attending the funeral in London on Wednesday. And as Wednesday is the first day of technical rehearsals in the theatre (lasting 'from 10.30 a.m. till whenever'), Rob has decided to find another operator. No easy task in three days.

To have this emergency compounded by the unannounced arrival of collaborators suddenly unable to reach a comparatively simple script agreement without dumping a hard-working and pleasant young actress only a week before opening, commendably produces no outward show of supreme annoyance.

Instead, in his usual calm, ruminative manner, Rob listens to Duncan's solution, then mine, makes careful pencil notes, rubs a few out, writes a few more, listens with admirable restraint to the compromise.

Finally, a decision of sorts. Mostly Duncan's stuff but with a trace of mine. His heifer at the beginning of Scene Ten, a fraction of me at the end of Scene Ten, the garage lines in Scene Eleven.

Duncan suggests we nip round to his office straight away, tap it into the word processor, get a print-out, drop it off to Rob on the way home. I attempt to negotiate my way out of this, because I am not convinced we have overcome the fragmentation problem, because I loathe not drafting and redrafting before typing, because Duncan is at home with the word processor and I am not, and because ... because I am becoming incoherent with exasperation.

We walk up the road towards the office, Duncan cross-examining me on my evident discontent, I foolishly persisting I am sunshine itself while struggling to find a way of acquitting myself honourably from my own unreasonable behaviour. This lasts some time. Once at the office, there's a lot of pacing about. Eventually, push myself into a semblance of amiability, taking the opening Duncan provides by giving me far more latitude than my mood justifies in the actual composition of the thing.

Monday 3   Nineteenth day of rehearsals. One
week to go.

Run-through. Fergus, the new lighting operator, Scots, tall, small ball of a head, short black hair brushed back, tracks through the marked cue script alongside Andrea, the sound operator, American, medium height, round face, short black hair diving forward.

'Okay,' says Rob, 'just concentrate on telling the story.'

Act One is cohesive, sure-footed. The jack-handle scene only just scrapes by, but its foundations are set now; give it time. Faith Geer is line-steady, although still tentative in places, but confident enough to begin mapping a performance. My God, the fright she gave us a week ago. And what tenacity she has in overcoming what must have been an intensely distressing time for her.

Casy, though, has slipped off in another direction. The wino has gone all right, loping and laughing into history, but the critical observer of people who had taken his place, someone fascinated by his own theories, open-minded enough to adapt them after the litmus-test of experience and finding as much curiosity in redefining them as he did in formulating them in the first place, has become too remote. The effect is that Casy seems indifferent to what is going on. And if Casy appears unconcerned, the audience will be equally uninvolved, for as well as watching a character in his own right, we are also watching a presiding influence and an interpreter of events.

But Peter Spears' performance is becoming steadily more authoritative. From the start an unruffled actor, I wondered at one stage whether his portrayal of Tom Joad might be a wholly intellectual one. It still veers that way. But now we are seeing a man conditioned by prison. Naturally open and easy-going – we see this in the opening scenes with his family, especially his brothers and sister – prison has taught him to be guarded with others. The rawness he needed in early rehearsals is now rooted in the knowledge that his emotions can still control his actions, and an abrasiveness towards strangers and those who hold power. Here is a man removed from a world he knew, suddenly thrust into alien territory. He has become prison-wise in his privacy, but not at ease with himself.

George and Peter have been rehearsing in quite different ways. George tends to go for full-blown effect, discarding what he doesn't need, storing away what he might; going again, discarding, storing away; Peter takes one small element at a time, then builds something else on to it, builds something more on to that . . .

Act Two still has its problems. It is broken in two by the dance sequence, in fact the Rose of Sharon–Old Woman scene, which will never play on stage because it doesn't work in the script. I now want to take it out entirely. Either side of this, the Act is shaping reasonably well, so the effect is of direction being regained after being blown badly off-course.

However, Duncan was right to insist we place the Al and Aggie relationship in two sections rather than my one. The heifer story has found its place at the beginning of Scene Ten, the few added lines between Al and Ma, then Ma and Pa, create time-scale, but the section at the end of Scene Ten – Al and Aggie making marriage plans – is still mawkish and insubstantial.

Mentioned this to Rob at the end of the run. He is enthusiastic for a re-write extending the scene. I still want to build up Aggie, creating some history for her, of her leaving home with her family, being on the road. Rob's suggestion is, do we now need to see them discussing marriage plans, as it robs us of the impact of our Scene Eleven re-write when Al tells Ma and Pa that he and Aggie intend to marry. Taking this out will leave me free to develop character.

Awkward few moments with Duncan after we pack up and Rob had disappeared. The scene, he says, does not need re-writing. I am conscious that I'm plunging us once again into an emotional stand-off, but insist that it does. Conversation becomes all the more tense as we are standing waiting on the street, Janet having agreed to meet us in the car and give us a lift home. By the time she arrives, I'm certain he'd rather travel alone, and I know I'd prefer to walk, but for him to mention this would only appear gratuitously rude, and for me to mention it would only appear gratuitously churlish. So, a silent and strained car journey with probably an understandably perplexed driver.

At the end of the run itself, there had been spontaneous applause for the actors. The first time this has happened. How hard they're working.

We're not there yet, but for a moment tonight everyone knew the play is beginning to turn the corner.

And then, minutes later, this. Another of those ridiculous fast rewinds from breakthrough to bitterness.

Tuesday 4   Now. I am writing this through clenched teeth. I have re-written the Al and Aggie end-of-Scene-Ten re-write in the same manner. My teeth, in other words, have been clenched most of the morning.

I have chucked out all the mawkish marriage stuff, and written a more deliberate, longer piece. It is one of Al and Aggie's regular evening rendezvous somewhere at the edge of the camp. They look down across the boxcars, supplemented now by makeshift tents and shelters crowded together. Aggie says that at night the camp, with its dotted lights, is almost as beautiful as a travelling fair. Al replies that he's heard more workers are due at the camp tomorrow and that the cotton will not last for long. Aggie has heard talk of a cotton-picking machine, which, if it caught on, will make hand-picking redundant. She reminisces about her life back home in Arkansas. They swap memories.

What Aggie does is widen the audience's vision from the Joads. Through her we catch a glimpse both of another family and the current industrial situation. It harkens back to the 'world view' of the beginning of the play. I'm convinced it is much more what is needed, though the manner in which I achieved it could have been improved upon, I suppose. Still. It'll resolve itself. Plough on . . .

Later: run-through. Chris Ann Moore has come up with two very good ideas, both for Act Two. The first is for the end of Scene One, as the lights go down on the destruction of Hooverville by Bird and the cops. In the couple of seconds of darkness as the sounds diminish, before the lights fade up on Scene Two, Weedpatch, Chris Ann suggests that Rose of Sharon twice calls for Connie. When the lights do come up, she is seen alone.

The second is for Scene Eleven, after she confesses her betrayal of Tom to Ma. Rose of Sharon's line, 'You ain't gonna whip me?' is throwing Chris Ann because she believes it is the wail of a frightened child and does not reflect the shame of a maturing woman. It effectively puts the clock of Rose of Sharon's development back, leaving her precious little time and material with which to make up ground and emerge credibly as the madonna she is at the end of the play.

She is quite right. The line is adapted from the novel, where 'Gonna whip her, Ma?' is the ten-year-old Winfield's hope when he tells Ma that twelve-year-old Ruthie is the traitor. It is absolutely wrong for Rose of Sharon. Chris Ann's suggestion is to replace the line with a simple 'I'm sorry'.

We incorporate both ideas.

But one thing I don't like in that section in Scene Eleven is Rose of Sharon's shamed allusion to having done 'hug-dancin'' with Connie in Sallisaw, a reference back to the Old Woman at Weedpatch, who warns Rose of Sharon that not only square-dancing but 'hug-dancin'' goes on at the Saturday night dances, and that a pregnant girl who had been 'hug-dancin'' subsequently 'dropped that baby dead'. It is such a small strand in Rose of Sharon's hysteria, that I'd like to cut it along with the Old Woman scene, but Rob likes the hug-dancing motif, and neither Chris Ann nor any of the other actors have said anything against it.

Act One in good shape tonight. Improvements on last night where needed, pace, rhythm locking in. Jack-handle scene there at last.

Act Two: Damien Kavanagh's Persky tends to zealously thump the table in front of him during his speech to the Bakersfield Association. However, my re-writing his speech to remove some of the more florid passages, 'the red flag of Communism', 'moral rot and disease' has had the fortunate bonus of reducing the table-shakers from three to one, the one being on 'it *can't* happen here'.

On two consecutive nights now, Tom has slipped in the word 'innocent' before 'guy' in the 'wherever they's a cop beatin' up a guy' line in his final speech. It'll have to go. It alters Tom's intentions and thought processes entirely.

The barn scene needs work. Ma, Pa, and Rose of Sharon go to the barn, on higher ground, to shelter from the flood. Ma screens her daughter with a blanket as she strips off her soaking dress. Rose of Sharon then wraps the blanket around herself. She briefly nods to Ma that she will help the Starving Man. Ma then takes Pa and the Barn Girl outside. Rose of Sharon kneels beside the man, takes him in her arms and pulls him on to her breast, raising her head to the audience and 'smiling mysteriously'.

At the moment, we are not seeing her nod of assent clearly, or enough of her face at the end. She tends to keep her back to us and her head down.

The running time of the play has been consistent for the past two run-throughs. Tonight is Act One – 59 minutes, 51 seconds; Act Two – 59 minutes, 45 seconds.

During the past few nights, Rob, Duncan, and I have evolved a routine of taking our dinner break at a small basement bistro in a street near the rehearsal room. It is cheap, the tables, crockery, and cutlery are clean, the food is simple and well-cooked, the staff civil, and – and this really clinches it – there is no music. Here we sit, analysing. Tonight, over mackerel and wine, Rob describes one of his conversations with Peter Spears, when he was searching for an image for Peter to consider in his playing of Tom. He suggested Peter approach the part, oddly enough, bearing in mind Clint Eastwood's 'man with no name' Western films. The Eastwood character, the stranger in town, keeps himself apart from others, is reserved yet powerful, cautious yet decisive. It must have struck a chord, for there is a seam of this enigmatic, almost aloof quality in Peter's performance now.

News from the Steppenwolf front. Frank Gelati, associate director of the Goodman Theatre, Chicago, and who is adapting *The Grapes of Wrath* for Steppenwolf, has booked a ticket to see the show on 14 August. I knew somebody representing Steppenwolf would come. But the writer . . . Would *I* want to see somebody else's version at the same time as doing my own . . .?

Rob broaches the subject of the curtain call. How is it going to be done? My choice is for the ensemble to come on together, bow once, then off. Should this be impractical (in other words, that all fifteen actors can't fit easily across a twenty-foot stage), then Barn Girl, Aggie, and the six actors playing more than one part should come on first, bow and off, and the remaining seven, Ma, Pa, Tom, Al, Rose of Sharon, Casy, and Connie, come on second, bow and off. Jodi, says Rob, goes for the first option. Apparently, on Broadway, where who comes on when, stands where, and takes how many bows at the curtain is far more important to the actors, their friends, their agents, their agents' friends, and whoever else happens to be around, than the actual show itself, it is the done thing for the director to duck out of organising the curtain and turn the whole ghoulish business over to his assistant, who can then be fired if he or she offends anyone's sensibilities.

Later: what has gone disgracefully unrecorded so far is the extraordinary amount of time and commitment Albert has given to this entire project, both as dramaturg and actor. Although Duncan and I initially found it difficult to adjust from a collaboration of two to being part of a larger group, however keenly we anticipated it, Albert applied his dramaturgical skills in those March script meetings with unfailing fortitude and generosity. Once rehearsals began in earnest, he stepped back from dramaturgical work with equal grace.

From the first, we had our reservations about Albert as Pa, something the read-through and first rehearsals did nothing to alleviate. Albert once said himself he would not be obvious casting as Pa. That might be so. But it is as if Albert has absorbed into his bearing and manner, drip by drip, a character. The drips have been – to me – imperceptible, but at recent run-throughs there has been more Pa than Albert, and tonight there was almost a complete transformation. His voice began harsh and then wearied, his eyes began bitter and became beaten, the body moved lightly at first, leadenly by the end. His pacing on his crucial first speech ('Ever' year we got a good crop comin' . . . ') was exactly right. The arc of the role was visible, not as sure-footed or as finely-textured as I hope it will be, but it was there and beginning to gel.

Albert's credits include Equity showcases and off-Broadway shows, TV soap operas and films, most recently a small part in Woody Allen's *The Purple Rose of Cairo*.

Wednesday 5   Twenty-first day of rehearsals, the first of technical rehearsals in the theatre. By the time I arrive, the auditorium is covered by a rubble of polythene sheeting, rolls of tarpaulin, trunks, barrels, and lights. More tarpaulin and bags of tools lie across seats, used paper-cups line the lip of the stage like a row of broken footlights and cables – bunched together by tape – snake down steps, over the backs of seats, around step-ladders and out through wedged-open doors.

Janet Scarfe is fitting the backcloth, the lighting operator is mooching about with the plans, and Graham Smith, the production stage manager, is repairing the back of an old chair with new wood, making it safe for Al to sit on when he tells the heifer story.

Rob stands silently in the back row, still radiating an air of calm, although an astute observer could recognise signs of tension: left palm cupping right elbow, right palm cupping chin; an instant and meticulously detailed summary of the vast amount that has not been achieved today rather than the very little that has (the preset – the state of sound and lights when the audience come into the theatre).

The backdrop – black with fuzzy ochre stripes across its lower section – creates the illusion of bringing the rear wall forward, something I had not foreseen. A scrim curtain of loose beige sacking, a giant map of the mid and west United States painted on it, is hung across the front of the stage. As the lights go up on the cast tableau, they will be seen through the scrim by the audience. Tom will make his opening speech standing in front of it, the following Tenant and Tractor Man pieces will be seen through it, and the Used-Car Salesman will do his piece from the small gallery above the audience on the right of the theatre before the scrim is drawn back by Tom for Scene Two.

'I got my map,' says Albert.

I'd prefer an open stage, I always prefer an open stage, but the scrim does look much better than I thought it would, although when Jodi demonstrates how easily Tom will be able to draw it back, walking quickly from stage left to stage right, the whole lot, including the rail holding it up, dips gracefully, then crashes unceremoniously to the floor.

'And look at it now,' says Rob.

The actors are pleased with the space, plotting their moves across the stage, staring purposefully into the front row, vanishing into dressing rooms, darting into entrances and exits, heading off into blind corners, following their noses in one direction, getting lost, and re-appearing looking bemused or self-satisfied, in another part of the theatre.

I give Rob the new Al and Aggie piece and push off home to my ignored dinner guests, who are quite happy being hosted by the ever-patient Vivien, and beginning their second courses and third bottle of wine.

Thursday 6   Allen Wright, arts editor of *The Scotsman*, rings. I have been one of his team reviewing the Festival for a couple of years, but I am in something of a dilemma as to whether I should be this year, being involved with a show myself. After a bit of backwarding and forwarding, we agree on my reviewing four or five official Festival productions – including readings by Soviet poets, one by Yevtushenko – and two or three on the Fringe during the first two weeks, but no American work of any kind.

The tech: to the theatre in the afternoon, to see how the technical rehearsal is getting on. The houselights are mostly off, but in the gloom the auditorium appears even more cluttered than it was yesterday. Rob sits in the second from back row with notepad and torch, wearing a set of headphones connected to a small microphone, and from which a long coiled flex leads to a loudspeaker in the lighting and sound box behind him. Every few seconds, to Rob's murmured instructions, the place is plunged into darkness, a light fades up on the stage, holds, then dies. Dribs and drabs of music seep from the stage speakers. The actors, in costume, sit about watching, standing on stage for lighting position and intensity checks when their scene is lit. It has obviously been, is, and is going to be a long and arduous process. To have three days teching a show on the Fringe, or the official Festival for that matter, is, however, a real luxury. Stage crews are annually the unrecognised stars of the Edinburgh Festival. But luxury is our necessity: over a hundred lighting cues and not an easy sound tape that has only just arrived from New York.

One problem now is the scrim, or rather the one-inch wide line of black emulsion representing Highway 66 painted horizontally across it, dividing it into halves, and ending, and this is clearly marked in copperplate lettering, in Beverly Hills, rather than following the Joads' turn-off across the desert to Bakersfield. Furthermore, its neck-high dips and humps, its pitch emphasis, fail to become transparent when the tableau light shines through them as the state lines do, but instead remain blatantly prominent, giving the disconcerting illusion that the Joads and others standing behind it are being decapitated before they even get on the road.

Long discussion on re-doing the scrim.

Meanwhile, try the fall-back, playing the tableau crouching. As Tom, too, now drops into a crouch (why?) for his 'Night after night . . .' speech and Pa's 'Ever' year . . .' has to be delivered in the same way, I have the depressing thought that the audience might deduce we're setting up a mad dramatic convention of doing the whole thing groping around on hands and knees. And it is so darkly lit, like a cave, so dark in fact, that the only part of Owner Man, the landowner who speaks in response to Pa (and who, at least, is standing), that is visible in that little tunnel of dim light, is his right foot. Pa, addressing him in turn, therefore yanks his head around to the right and protests into utter blackness, out of which comes a voice some way above an eerily moving ankle and shoe.

The backdrop worries me as well. Its blackness. Everything is black.

Later: to a press party to herald the Festival, held at a large commercial modern art gallery in a restored Old Town warehouse. The building next door, taken over by the gallery, has been converted into a theatre, and a mostly female band called the Jam Tarts kick up a raucous racket on a five-foot high stage in a vast high-ceilinged room. The sound quality is appalling. The man who emerges from the crowd with a bottle of wine and fills my glass, introduces himself as Robert Patrick. The American author of *Kennedy's Children*, that dark, acidic play about the crushing personal price folk heroes can pay for their heroism, is here to première a new play, *The Last Stroke*, about the emotional turmoil of an abstract expressionist painter, not a million miles removed from Jackson Pollock and, like *Kennedy's Children*, set in a last-post New York bar. Robert Patrick is a tall, middle-aged, genially overweight man, wiry grey hair spilling across his forehead and broad, kind face, and wearing comfortably dishevelled tee-shirt and green fatigues. He has calculated that should the play flop, he and the cast of two will only lose about £5,000, and says that to risk so little, in comparison to what would be at stake even off-Broadway, makes the trip to Edinburgh worth while.

Friday 7 Posters for Fringe shows are going up all over Edinburgh, though none have appeared, nor is there any hint of any appearing, for *The Grapes of Wrath*. Some Fringe shows have already opened, although the Festival does not start until Monday and the crowds are thin. Hal's Reader's Digest window has nothing in it except Reader's Digest do-it-yourself manuals, road atlases, and a range of, I think cut-price, luggage. There is nothing outside the Netherbow Theatre to indicate the show is to open, and the Depression photographs have not, as yet, materialised.

There is an American Festival Theatre publicity girl somewhere, although her whereabouts are as unknown to me as her publicity, the point of which, the derivation of the word, surely, is that it is public.

Saturday 8 Twenty-fourth and final day of re-hearsals. Once, oh, long ago, months ago, it was hazarded that tonight would be a preview, at which an audience might see the show for a reduced price. However, debilitating hazards have intervened since – not least among them that even now re-writing is still being done – and the public preview has been reduced to a private dress rehearsal.

Just as well. Lighting cues are fractionally late and sound cues even later. The acting is uneven and the performance uninteresting, due both to the cast being almost overwhelmingly tired (several are rehearsing one other show, some have the pressure of two openings on Monday, and others an opening on Tuesday), and their evident need now to get this show in front of an audience and get a lift from them. I hope they get both. The audience and the lift.

We cut the few lines after Casy's death, which the tightening-up of this sequence now render superfluous. The scene now ends with Casy's 'You don' know what you're doin'' to the advancing Hooper's Ranch guards, his raising his arm to protect himself from their clubs, and a snap blackout. Cutting the slow motion fall in red light rescues the scene from the melodramatic and makes it emblematic. It does, though, mean an extra line for Ma in the following scene. Ten days ago I'd have thought twice about this. Tonight Faith adjusts instantly.

Interesting the way the actors adapt to the theatre. For some, like David Beggs and Temple Williams, it is a simple process of transferring their rehearsal room work to another space, of packing up their performances and unpacking them somewhere else. Others, like George, seem suddenly uncertain of how the script might work and test it out all over again, playing odd lines almost in capital letters, and quite unnecessarily gesturing through sub-text. Albert, by contrast, appears muted, as if he is wary of the stage. But Faith and Chris Ann take on new life. Faith is almost proprietorial, ranging across the stage, becoming ever more authoritive. The apple-cheeked Mom has gone. Chris Ann is very strong, the development in Rose of Sharon, what Rob calls 'from brat to earth mother', begins to take on a stature. And she gives us the ending: the assent and the head up. And, utterly surprising and for the first time, tears. A great step forward for her.

Afterwards, more lengthy notes. Rob makes a speech about what has been achieved, tacking on little codas about what still has to come. Only once does the Rob benevolence slip, and then it is not directed at an actor but at Jodi who, busy packing some equipment, is not listening to what he is saying.

'. . . you agree, Jodi?'

'I'm sorry?'

'Yes, I'm sorry, too.'

It is gone in a moment, but a barb of tension showed and it chilled.

Once the actors have packed up and gone, Rob, Jodi, the lighting operator, Graham, Duncan, and I work laboriously on, tracking our way through Rob's entire lighting design, light by light, state by state, Graham and I standing in for the actors on the stage, in a final push to get this show technically right. I can contribute little to this other than standing in various spots. I am happier at actors' rehearsals, watching, adjusting script, listening to their thoughts and ideas; Duncan, with a vast back-up of experience which I don't have, is far more at home in technicals. He has an extraordinarily precise stage and technical eye. He moves now with Rob between the auditorium and the lighting box, organising, quietly suggesting refinements, perfecting, all with infinite patience and great skill. Finally the lights are set.

At 1.30 in the morning, as we walk out of the theatre and into the yellow-lit deserted street, damp greasing the cobbles, and turn up towards the Castle esplanade where flags hang limply from their poles, we discuss the Rose of Sharon–Old Woman scene. Failing any brilliant ideas between now and lunchtime, Rob, Duncan, and I agree it should go. Rob has the unenviable task, then, of telling Dorothy Bernard that she has lost her second role in the play only the day before we open.

I feel past tiredness. I feel past most things.

Sunday 9   Glancing back through last night's, or this morning's, entry, I can see that it conflicts, describing the performance as uneven and uninteresting, then going on to say how impressive some of the cast were. Really, it is less an accurate report of last night's events than a sketch of my own state. If I sit down and think about it, I don't know how an audience will respond to this play. I know what I originally hoped some of the responses would be. I wanted the play to move, sadden, uplift. But daily repetition leads to immunity and now I look at some of the lines and wonder what people will think.

Morning: with Vivien to the Book Festival, a marquee village pitched on the grass beneath the trees in Charlotte Square, in the New Town, to hear an interview with P.D. James, author of the Adam Dalgleish and Cordelia Gray detective novels. Masterly fiction, forensically detailed yet written with great insight and compassion.

She is a small, homely, direct, bespectacled woman in a print dress whose greatest literary influences, she says, are Jane Austen, Dorothy L. Sayers, and Graham Greene. Her ideas derive not from an incident or a character, either real or imagined, but from place. The fens of East Anglia or, in the case of *A Taste For Death*, a church. An enthusiastic explorer of old churches, she was browsing one day in an Oxfordshire vestry, with its piles of split prayer books, dust, and smell of furniture polish, when she had the idea of the discovery of two men lying there, dead in 'a welter of blood'. The vestry and the bodies were subsequently moved to Paddington.

Before beginning her first novel, she had to decide whether her detective was to be a professional or an amateur, and chose a professional – Adam Dalgleish – for reasons of realism, the author not only having to provide the amateur with a coincidental reason for being in the right place at the right time, but also a reason to be consulted by the police to solve the crime, which, in these days of forensic analysis, is remote. 'Just imagine,' she says, eyes glinting behind the spectacles, 'if a man in the centre of the sixth row was to suddenly slump forward with a knife in his back, it would be highly unlikely that the dozen people sitting around him would each have a significant but separate reason to kill him, or that Scotland Yard would wish to resort to my services in finding the murderer.' She sounds almost disappointed.

The difference between the detective novels of the 1930s and 1940s and those of today is that in the former, the denouement represents a restoration of order, while in the latter, everyone and everything is in some way changed by death. As in le Carré's spy fiction, order is never quite restored and never to what it was.

Later: phone call from Rob. An idea, he says, for the Rose of Sharon–Old Woman scene that will kill two birds with one stone. He suggests asking Heather Hitt to replace Dorothy Bernard and play the part as a young, rather distressed girl. One of the problems with the scene as it stands is that the audience might read it that in some obscure way the ghost of Granma had returned to haunt Rose of Sharon. God, I hadn't thought of that . . . If Heather plays it, he adds, the dubiety would be eliminated. It would not read so contrary to the conventions of the play, but be sufficiently disturbing to work, in one sense, as a kind of narration, as Rose of Sharon's inner voice. Second, he proposes that instead of being played, as now, immediately before the Tom–Al–Higgins scene, it is played immediately after it, giving the dance sequence a harder ending and creating a clearer through-line for Rose of Sharon's hysteria.

I think this could work. It's certainly a vast improvement. It'll mean re-cueing lights and re-staging work, but Rob assures me it can be done in time for tomorrow. And it means Heather learning the lines, of course. No problems there, says Rob, she's a fast worker. She'll have to be. Poor girl. From having almost been written out of the entire show last Sunday, she's had nothing but new and more lines given to her all week, and very little rehearsal time. I tell him to go ahead and promise to take the responsibility of telling Duncan.

Catch him in after getting no answer a couple of times. As I should have guessed, he doesn't like the idea (or my solo authorisation of it), objecting on the grounds of staging difficulties, which I'm happy to leave Rob to overcome, and that there is so little time to rehearse it, something again I'm happy to leave to Rob's judgement. He'd rather just cut the Old Woman scene. Or Young Girl scene, whichever it is.

Ring Rob to report. Instead, got Hal, busy typing programmes. Rob has gone off somewhere, didn't say where. Ring Duncan back to bring him up to date. A rather strained conversation but agree to give Rob free passage to do his best.

With Vivien to see the Mexican Compagnie di Divas in *Donna Giovanni*, a free adaptation of *Don Giovanni*, at the Assembly Rooms. Five young women and one man, each of whom plays the Donna, or the Don, at various points (whoever wears the pony-tail), and singing to piano accompaniment. Minimal setting, bare stage (and all the women at times with bare breasts), movement and images taken from Renaissance paintings. Thoroughly entertaining.

On to *Company*, an adaptation of the Samuel Beckett novel, icily performed by Julian Curry, meticulously and vibrantly directed by Tim Pigott-Smith at Richard Demarco's tiny black shoebox of a theatre in a crumbling building still being restored.

Well. We open tomorrow.

Monday 10   No phone calls this morning. Why?

Go up to the theatre to arrive just before three, so as to avoid hanging about once I'm there, having worked out that if I get there with only moments to spare I could unobtrusively nip in, see the show, and then nip off to the pub with any of the company who happen to be about, rather than hang around the foyer beforehand, doing nothing except feeling terrified.

Meet Duncan by chance outside. He's striding so purposefully down the street towards me, I thought perhaps he was actually making a getaway and hoping I might not notice, but in fact he'd been hovering about on the kerb, distraught that I had not arrived, and had caught sight of me before I him.

The performance is sold out. Not only is it sold out, it is sold out with no advertising posters around town, no Reader's Digest shop-window, no Depression photographs at the theatre, nothing at the theatre at all save a proof poster hurriedly put up this morning and now flapping from one pin in the summer breeze. Not only is it sold out, we have so far turned about thirty people away and some of those have bought tickets for tomorrow.

I never imagined this. I thought we might begin quietly, take this week to build, and perhaps do well next week.

The foyer is packed. Owen Dudley Edwards, reader in American history at Edinburgh University, polymath, and critic, is here reviewing the play for *The Scotsman*. He is a critic for whose opinions I have deep respect, which are always enlightening, trenchant, and frequently spiked with wit and word-play. Sue Ellen is here, looking photogenic after hours of work on the costumes, taking all the ruffles out of Rose of Sharon's dress, modifying other costumes, changing some completely, distressing them all. Rob looks composed and reassuring in, or perhaps because of, the light grey sports jacket he's wearing and the document case he carries under his arm. Hal, in a brown suit, even in a crowd is whisking here and there doing several things at once.

An announcement that we're going to be late going up. In fact, ten minutes late going up. Compulsory inspection of the electrics, or something. All my tactical planning for my time of arrival, and I'll have to hang about after all. Edge outside with Duncan. No mutiny in the crowd yet, but there's a bit of talk about a French play at a wash-house round the corner due to start at the same time as us. I worry our cast will be unsettled by the delay and will then have their work cut out reviving a disgruntled audience. They probably won't be at all unsettled, of course. It's me that's unsettled. Supremely unsettled. Which I wasn't before this. I was absolutely calm walking up the road.

I wish I knew how the actors *felt*. I know how I feel, and imagine how Duncan feels. We have, after all, collaborated in writing this play for a year, through all the sketches, rejects, drafts, re-workings, and re-writes, but I can't predict anyone's reaction to this last-moment unforeseen delay. The actors might be more nervous. They might not.

At last, at 3.15, a quarter of an hour late, the preset lights and the music fade down, the tableau lights and the wind sound fade up, and there is the first glimpse of the defeated sharecroppers huddled over the dead earth. One draws his hand across the ground in front of him and lets the barren dust run through his fingers – Rob once again drawing a virtue out of a necessity.

I'm sitting in the third row, Duncan is watching from the lighting box. I sense that the opening, the cameos of Tom, tenants, Owner Man, Tractor Man, and the Used-Car Salesman, takes the audience somewhat by surprise, as if they do not recognise what they thought they might see.

The scrim draws back safely. Lighting makes a profound impact on a set design. The lighting in this show delineates time and place as much as anything else, and Janet Scarfe's set provides for this in a way I had not imagined before. She has made a series of very appropriate choices in the austerity of her design and its painterly, rough-and-ready quality.

Casy seems a little tense, but Tom's admission of the crime that landed him in jail is the best he has ever played it, ashamed of nothing, squaring up to the former preacher, yet no hint of threat in his voice. Casy steadies and the first Act is strong, the Casy–Tom balance emerging well and Ma controlling the jack-handle scene, an Act One litmus-test, superbly. The lights streaming on to the audience at the end as the family stand and gaze for the first time across the valley and into California, create a fantasy of sun-filled hope. Their snapping out, and – Rob's idea – Matt Gallagher's Texan (the returning migrant Casy talks to at Needles), sitting at the side of the stage and lighting a cigarette, the match flaring in the darkness and illuminating his face, undercuts the dream with a poignant premonition of the reality to come.

As the house lights go up, a pause broken by healthy applause. Nip up to the back of the auditorium and through the door, to find Rob and Duncan outside the lighting box.

Rob: 'S.F.S.G.'

'What?'

'So far, so good.'

Act Two, to me the more difficult, begins with the house lights up, Deputy Sheriff Bird calling the Bakersfield Association (we, the audience) to order. Duard Mosley has to do a bit of good-natured chivvying of late-comers, but it's taken in good heart.

The new Rose of Sharon–Young Girl scene is a transformation in terms of pace and staging, and nobody would guess that Heather has been given so little time in which to rehearse it, but to me the dance sequence, the news of the cops outside the gate, the interrogation of Higgins, the dialogue between Rose of Sharon and the girl, is still the weakest in the play. This is because, it occurs to me now, and only now, it is inconclusive. Nothing actually *happens* on stage. Every other sequence works towards or centres around a specific statement. Not this one. I know why it is there. It is intended to show the increasing social responsibility of Tom, the ability of the Joads to act as part of and in relation to a larger group, and provide psychological motivation for Rose of Sharon. The points are made, but only elusively so.

The audience seem to enjoy the Ma and Pa confrontations. Pa's 'Come time we settle down, I aim to smack her one,' gets a sympathetic laugh; Ma's reply, 'Come that time, you can. Now, roust up', a bigger one, and both go better than the heifer story. Rob and Albert were right. The audience does look for humour and the encroaching tragedy does need something to play against. But the quality of the humour rests in the responses of the characters, in recognisable human foibles rather than jokey anecdotes.

The flood sequence is confidently sustained and the ending, Rose of Sharon, a woman suffering yet noble, hunched over the Starving Man, the rain hammering on the roof of the barn, is played with great authority and Chris Ann Moore is, to me, intensely moving. The audience are absolutely still, absolutely silent. It is a silence that remains throughout Tom's final 'I'll be there' speech, the lights dying, the rain sound welling up and then snapping abruptly off.

A very warm audience response.

Later, in a café-pub up the road profiting substantially by our patronage, we buy all the cast drinks. It has been a very good opening: Peter Spears' Tom, subtle and commanding; George McGrath's Casy, complex and humanitarian; and Faith Geer's Ma, a devastating portrayal of a woman of great inner strength refusing to be subjugated by physical hardship and emotional distress – at the end, Ma is battered by misfortune but her spirit is defiant and proud. The credit belongs to the actors and Rob. To say that he has brought the play in on time sounds banal, but he has wrought an ensemble from fifteen individuals, maintained his own timetable and the equilibrium of rehearsals by his stability, clear-sightedness, and logic. He has coped with innumerable anxieties and, as have the actors, with four weeks of re-writes. Whatever the fate of the play during the next three weeks, he and the actors have done a remarkable job. The lot of the actors is, they have to keep on doing it.

Tuesday 11   Last night a flurry of openings launched the Festival and Fringe, among them, as part of the Festival World Theatre Season – an innovation created last year by Festival director, Frank Dunlop – the Gate Theatre Company from Dublin in Sean

O'Casey's *Juno and the Paycock*, a production of painstaking pictorial naturalism.

With *The Grapes* having opened but the Festival and Fringe not yet into their stride and the city still not that crowded, I feel a sense of being somewhat cut adrift. Today, though, a curious juxtaposition of East and West.

The East: this morning to a Festival reading by two Soviet poets, which I'm reviewing for *The Scotsman*. Verses read first in Russian by their authors and then in English by a translator, satirical but not subversive pieces about labyrinthine bureaucracy, lyrical pieces about fields and linden trees. Afterwards, a woman in the audience asks one of the Russians whether it is possible to buy his book in this country.

'I give you this one.'

'No, really, I would like to buy a copy.'

'No,' says the poet stoically, 'I give you this one. Sometimes books sent from my country to your country . . . get lost. There are ways we have of being sure they will arrive, but simple for me now to give you this one.'

The West: to a midnight reception for the entire American Festival Theatre company at the Royal Scots Club. All the AFT shows have now opened, *The Grapes of Wrath*, *Hot l Baltimore* and *Come Back to the Five and Dime, Jimmy Dean, Jimmy Dean* yesterday, and *Stage Door* and *University* tonight. *Hot l* and *Stage Door* had good audiences and there was another full house for *The Grapes* today, although, according to Albert, the performance lacked the freshness of yesterday.

There is bread, cheese, even champagne; whoopings and hugs and camera flashes popping. Rob has a batch of *The Grapes of Wrath* posters, which have just been delivered. The design is similar to the drawing on the Press releases, black on a white ground, a pen and ink sketch of a man standing alone on a road, his back to the viewer, gazing towards a cloud of dust fuzzing the horizon. Simple and direct. Come across Karen St Pierre, the public relations girl, who explains the unexpected difficulty she has had in getting the Depression photographs out of Washington. She expects to hear good news anytime now, as she has a senator working on it for her.

'Shoulda called up Ollie North,' sings a voice.

Enthusiastic chorus of 'Woh! Too right! Hoo-ee . . .!'

What these disparate events tell anyone about the great imperial powers of our time, I don't know, except that they are quirkily indicative of current television and newspaper images of the two countries as bureaucrat and buccaneer. In Moscow, General Secretary Gorbachev, habitually dressed in a solemn grey suit, lugubriously and lengthily proclaims *glasnost*, 'openness', to an apparently unimpressed people; in Washington, Colonel Oliver North, compact, thrust-jawed, and neat in his military uniform, promises with barely-controlled emotion to 'tell it all', the altering and shredding of documents in the name of duty, to the televised circus of the Iran–Contra hearings, while outside the committee building demonstrators jig placards urging him to 'Go For it', and to run for president.

Wednesday 12   No review of *The Grapes* has appeared in *The Scotsman* as yet. To the theatre after the show to record an interview about the play with Rob and Paul Binotto for BBC Radio Scotland's *Good Morning, Scotland* programme. Tonight, with Vivien, Rob, and Albert to the Gorky Theatre of Leningrad's *Uncle Vanya*, effortlessly played and exquisitely staged, first performed in this production in 1982 and probably rehearsed for years before that. The director, Georgy Tovstonogov, a man with the profile of a buzzard, sits bolt-upright in a box close to the stage, wreathed in Socialist awards, People's Artist of the USSR, Laureate of Lenin, Hero of Socialist Labour . . .

Thursday 13   Edinburgh has so far been sluggish, but by midday today crowds are choking the Assembly Rooms and people are standing a dozen deep watching the jugglers, fire-eaters, and buskers on the wide paved walkway between Princes Street and the Playfair Steps alongside the Royal Scottish Academy draped with banners for the Saatchi Collection of Art exhibition. Theatre and concert-goers from home and abroad and people in the profession are arriving in the city by the hour. Journalists and critics from all around the world scurry about, plastic Festival Press packs clutched in their hands. Does half of whatever is written ever find its way back to the performing companies? The Festival is beginning to take wing and word-of-mouth is already circulating about the best Fringe shows to see. A lot of people are talking about *Hauptmann*, John Logan's play about the man convicted and executed in 1936 for kidnapping the Lindbergh baby. Performed by the Stormfield Theatre Company of Chicago, it has already won several American awards and looks set to do well here.

Although the main Festival has a loose Russian theme this year, the international, and particularly American, presence on the Fringe is stronger than ever.

With Vivien to see *The Grapes* this afternoon. Another full house and advance bookings are going very well. See Rob and the actors briefly before the show begins. They are pleased with Owen Dudley Edwards' *Scotsman* review, which appeared this morning, describing the script as 'at once faithful to the novel and yet absolutely a play in its own right', and Faith Geer as building 'the self-discovery of Ma Joad into the figure of power and wisdom that rightly invites comparison with O'Casey's Juno'.

A tight, muscular performance, the actors pacing the emotional arc much more confidently, having played in front of four audiences. They're now taking two bows instead of one at the end.

Friday 14   As I made no diary entry for the following at the time, this is being written in retrospect for the sake of continuity.

Yesterday we heard from the Fringe office that *The Grapes of Wrath* is to be given a *Scotsman* Fringe First award. I was astonished, and honoured, that the play had been judged worthy of ranking alongside the seven other winners: The Open Stage, Yugoslavia, for *Tattoo Theatre*; Stormfield Theatre Company, Chicago, for *Hauptmann*; Dominique Durvin and Helene Prevost, France, for *Le Lavoir*; Gcina Mhlope, Thembi Mtshali, and Maralin Vanrenen, South Africa, for *Have You Seen Zandile?*; Chorus Theatre, India, for *Chakravyuha*; Communicado Theatre Company, Scotland, for *Mary Queen of Scots Got Her Head Chopped Off*; and Richard Crane and Faynia Williams, England, for *Pushkin*.

The awards – wooden-framed copper plaques – were presented today at a lunchtime buffet-do at the Fringe Club by the actor Tom Watson, who gave a remarkable performance in Sam Shepard's *Fool For Love* at the National Theatre in 1984, and who is appearing in a new play, *A Wholly Healthy Glasgow*, by Iain Heggie, in the Festival this week.

I was, and still am, immensely pleased for Hal and Rob, whose company has now produced plays that have won awards in two successive years, and for *The Grapes* actors and crew.

Later, to the Yevtushenko reading at the King's Theatre. It is less of a reading, more of a performance. Yevtushenko the troubadour showman, pacing the stage, shoulders hunched and hands rammed deep into his pockets, or standing absolutely still with his arms held out from his sides, now growling his poetry, now chanting; swigging milk while the actor Nigel Hawthorne reads in translation, revelling in his applause and grinning, and in this case a cliché is perfectly accurate, exactly like the Cheshire Cat in Tenniel's illustration. Yevtushenko has been the Festival's visible Russian, popping up everywhere, dropping into pubs. 'Comrade Yevtushenko', as Albert calls him, even went to a performance of *Stage Door*.

A wizened paragraph on *The Grapes* in the *Guardian* today, tagged on to a fulsome review of the *Mary Queen of Scots* play, written by the *Guardian's* Scottish reviewer. Her angle on *The Grapes* is that it is 'a messy, flawed' (but fails to say in what way) 'but deeply emotional dramatisation'. The book is 'given a decent adaptation' ('decent', presumably, means adequate but uninspired), and performed 'by a young American company' (which implies the actors are miscast for age which, in the case of the principals, is utterly incorrect).

In fact, the thing is so perfunctorily written and contradictory, I have difficulty fathoming exactly what she's driving at. Unfortunately, Michael Billington, the paper's chief theatre critic, who writes lucid, well-reasoned stuff whether he applauds the play or production in question or not, devotes himself primarily to covering the Festival and mostly delegates the Fringe to others.

Tonight to Folkopera of Stockholm's Festival production of *The Magic Flute*. This company is one of Frank Dunlop's great discoveries, and last year created a sensation with their small-scale *Aida*. At home, they perform in an old 528-seat cinema. Here, they set up their stage in Leith Town Hall, and use the aisles and climb up and down steps built from the stage to the balconies as well. For this production the stage is a tilted disc of thick wire mesh with a semi-circular wall at the rear that hydraulically rises up and over to reveal the Queen of the Night. The costumes are from fairy tale (bright pastel jerkins and leggings for Papageno and Papagena) to the brutal modern (Sarastro in a beige foreman's coat at a bank of dials and levers). The orchestra is tucked beneath the stage, so nothing separates the singers from the audience. It is colourful, innovative, vibrant, and brilliant.

Saturday 15   Duncan and I have a meeting this
morning with Frank Gelati at his hotel. It is a small, gloomy place with
ageing wallpaper and dark woodwork, out of the city centre. We sit,
Duncan and I, in a bar that smells of last night's alcohol and this
morning's furniture polish, waiting for something to happen, while
someone trundles a vacuum cleaner across trodden-down carpet in the
shadows at the other end of the room.

Frank Gelati saw the play yesterday. It was, apparently, a good
performance. He arrives, a big, square-set man with a frost of short
silver-grey hair and beard, wearing a short-sleeved shirt over light
trousers. The vacuum cleaner chap brings coffee, and the three of us
talk about Steinbeck in general, move on to *The Grapes of Wrath* in
particular, this and that aspect, and the transference or non-
transference of this or that from the novel to the play. Fencing, really. It
feels rather odd to be discussing your own adaptation with someone
about to write, or already writing (which, is a bit hazy) his, especially
when that person is to write it for Steppenwolf and is associate director
of one of Chicago's leading theatres. I feel, therefore, both cautious and
privileged.

He is complimentary about the adaptation, particularly the extending
of Connie and Rose of Sharon, and closely questions other script
decisions. We spend some time talking about the non-naturalistic
qualities in the script and the production; his feeling is that one or two of
the younger actors are too inexperienced to bring out the full weight of
their roles. I agree this is a problem, but it would be a problem to be
overcome with any script and any production of *The Grapes*. Steinbeck's young people are very young – teenagers – and it would be
extremely difficult to find teenage actors able to carry the emotional,
psychological, and technical demands required for those characters.
Rob has taken the right direction to try to solve this by casting slightly
over-age.

Frank Gelati's idea at present is to write a mammoth adaptation to be
produced over three evenings: the first, Tom returning home from
McAlester; the second, the journey from Oklahoma to California; the
third, the events in California. The book logically breaks down into
these sections, sure enough, but it would require a massive amount of
money to stage a piece on that scale. And for the audience, there is the
risk of the problem I found with *The Henrys* in March. Nine hours is a
long time . . .

I learn a lot about theatre in America and especially about the workings of the Goodman in Chicago, where they have a team of fund-raisers who tot up over 1.5 million dollars a year . . .

Sunday 16   This morning, with Vivien and Graham Smith to *Hamlet*, performed, in Russian, by the Moscow Studio Theatre of the South West, at the Assembly Rooms, and which I am reviewing for *The Scotsman*. They are reputedly Moscow's leading fringe company and the interest, apart from the fact of it being a Russian *Hamlet*, is to see what is thought of in the Soviet Union as being experimental and innovative.

The answer, on the slim evidence of this one production, is what we might have thought of as experimental and innovative about fifteen years ago. Hamlet, gaunt in black, red hair down to his shoulders, has a propensity to lean arms folded against the speakers at either side of the stage that intermittently pump high-volume rock music, and is monotonously recalcitrant, of surly rather than antic disposition. Apart from almost hysterically gabbling his lines, there are no other signs of his slipping into madness, either feigned or otherwise. The other actors stand dotted about like chess pieces under overhead spotlights, facing the audience, bobbing up and down on the balls of their feet and shouting whenever the blasts of music threaten to obliterate what they are saying. The soliloquies are shortened, 'To be or not to be' transposed to precede the final duel between Hamlet and Laertes, which is fought to a barrage of disco music.

I can see the idea in the production, to show a dark, monolithic state feeding off its own corruption, but the point is the text already does this itself, very well. And there seems to be little text work in terms of meaning and delivery. As it is in Russian, I may be wrong, although the values seem primarily visual and aural. I can also see that this kind of treatment might be vigorously radical in the Soviet Union. But hardly here.

Depressing news tonight. While I am out, Vivien takes a call from Hal who says that Rob has to return to New York. He had planned to be in Edinburgh for the entire Festival but has unexpectedly had to rearrange his schedule. I feel very disappointed. I had come to rely on Rob's insight and reassurance, and I'm sure the cast had, too.

Monday 17   Heavy rain. To the theatre at 2.30 to
see Jodi, who now takes over the day-to-day running of the show. Rob
gave the actors notes after the performance when needed, and she will
be doing that as well as overseeing the technical side of things with
Graham for the remaining two weeks of the run.

Also to record an interview with the BBC World Service arts
programme, *Meridian*. An earnest looking woman with bobbed hair and
a thin face. Not having yet seen the play, which, if her reactions are
similar to the *Guardian* woman's, is a distinct piece of luck, she asks
straightforward, basic questions, how did you get the rights, find the
company, decide which characters to use and which not . . . The thing
is, the character stuff was such a long time ago, I have difficulty
remembering, but it seems to turn out all right. A tousled chap sits in
with us (we have commandeered an administrative office), who says that
he has never read the book. Suddenly alarmed, I ask him whether he is
reviewing the play. 'Oh, no,' he says, 'just . . . you know . . .' and nods
abstractly at the woman, who is checking to see if the tape-recorder will
reproduce my voice and whatever it is that I said, which I have now
forgotten. That's all right. I'm rather sensitive about doing an interview
and puffing the cast, only to be followed on air by someone saying he
thought they were lousy. Especially someone who has never read the
book.

Downstairs in the foyer, another full house waits for the auditorium
doors to open and a queue forms for any returned tickets. We have sold
out every day so far and bookings are healthy for a few days ahead. The
award has certainly helped us as it has others: *Hauptmann* is now very
difficult to get into and *Pushkin*, due to finish a one-week run last
Saturday, has transferred to another theatre and is doing well.

Hal, as always, zipping about. He does front of house for three AFT
shows a day, plus an enormous amount of administrative and dogsbody
work morning and night, not only looking after his own company but
also advising and assisting the other American companies at the Royal
Scots Club. Somehow he stays enviably fit and sane.

Spot a chap with an AFT Press pack. Hal is busy doing something or I
would have asked him who the chap was but instead, against my better
judgement, attempt casual amiability without introducing myself and
ask where he is from.

'*Kaleidoscope.*'

The BBC Radio 4 arts magazine programme. They are based in
London, but have an office in Edinburgh during the Festival. I am due

to review the Berliner Ensemble production of *Troilus and Cressida* for them on Wednesday. I ask him if he knew when they plan to review *The Grapes*.

'Oh, we might not,' he says. 'I mean, we usually just review new stuff.'

I could have asked him why, if the play was not going to be reviewed (I had eclipsed the 'might' as soon as it was said), the programme was bothering to send somebody along, but instead, as lightly as possible, say something to the effect that the adaptation *is* new. It is a world première. Says so on all the posters. (The posters are now up, incidentally, and have been a few days. Outside the theatre, inside the Reader's Digest window, a few other places.) And in the programme.

A slight pause. Then.

'Ah, but the *book's* not new, is it?'

The audience is in, the preset lights about to go down, when the bloke from BBC Radio Scotland's daily *Festival View* programme hurtles into the foyer out of the rain. He teaches music at a local further education college and usually reviews musicals. Well, he's just missed most of the music in this.

'Right, then,' he says, to anyone and everyone still in the foyer – Hal, the box-office girl, the disappointed few people in the returns queue – stomping wetly about, dragging a hank of damp hair away from his eyes, 'Which way do I go for this?'

And Hal does not flinch, but gently shows him the door marked THEATRE.

Later, Jodi reports a good performance. One of the trunks came apart, not at a crucial moment, and it is reasonable, I suppose, that a Joad trunk could collapse at some point. Reasonable, but not dramatically necessary.

Tonight, to *Troilus and Cressida*. The Berliner Ensemble is the company founded by Bertolt Brecht in East Berlin in 1949. Ekkehard Schall, married to Brecht's daughter Barbara, is playing Thersites in this production.

The design is sparse, a vast white sheet hanging down from above the stage which, manoeuvred this way and that, becomes a balcony of Pandarus's house, the entrance to the Greek camp, or – a moon and clouds projected on to it – a night sky. Pandarus becomes a civil servant figure, a power-broker fascinated by war while Thersites is bullish and cynical (too much so), rampaging against the Greeks, the Trojans, and war itself. The production emphasises less the destruction of romantic love than the destruction of culture by war.

Tuesday 18   8 a.m. Phone call from Owen Dudley Edwards. He is presenting a one-hour programme on the Festival and Fringe for BBC Radio Ulster and the producer, Chris Spurr, has invited me to take part in the half-hour discussion section. Several others will also be contributing and, having finished all my reviewing for *The Scotsman*, I'm looking forward to it. The programme is due to be broadcast live from Edinburgh on Saturday.

The phone call is to arrange a schedule of Fringe shows of Irish interest for me to see, for Owen to brief me on what else he wants to cover – Gate Theatre of Dublin, Berliner Ensemble – and to confirm a Friday lunch date at which all the contributors will meet. As always, Owen is on brilliant form: an effervescence of information, quotes (from James Joyce to Michael Billington), recommendations, warnings, gossip, and anecdote crackles through the telephone wire.

I begin my rounds with a play at Richard Demarco's this morning. Stopped at the door afterwards by one of the actors anxious to know where and when my review will appear. It being Radio Ulster means, of course, that he will not be able to hear it in Edinburgh. I understand his frustration when several reviewers come to see a play and the company has precious little to show for it.

Probably because of this, and my BBC encounters yesterday (I shall never approach a reviewer – or non-reviewer – off my own bat again), I am becoming increasingly disgruntled by the lack of notices from critics who have been to see *The Grapes*. *The Independent* came on Friday, but so far nothing has appeared in the paper, and there was nothing from the musicals bloke on *Festival View* this morning. The *Evening News* has promised to come – even booked a ticket once, I think – but has not, to my knowledge, shown up yet.

I feel odd about my reacting like this. As a reviewer myself, I know critics often don't have much control over when their stuff will appear. Or, especially during the Festival, even how much of it will appear, as several Fringe plays are often reviewed in one article that might then be cut for space by sub-editors. But as someone involved with a show, knowing this doesn't make me feel any better when reviewers come along and there is no apparent return. Or rather, no return within a certain time. Such as this morning, for the musicals bloke.

I don't even mind that much what the reviews say. Well, I do. I want them to be informed and discursive, and preferably favourable but if not, then at least informed and discursive. Not like the *Guardian* woman's, in other words.

Hal thinks I'm being impatient.

Adline Finlay of Chappell Plays came to see *The Grapes* today, having flown up to see us, the first British production of Arthur Miller's *Two-Way Mirror*, and a couple of other things. Her views on *The Grapes* are that it is an excellent script that could be developed to include more from the book, such as the episode in Chapter 15 of the travellers buying bread from a roadside diner, and reinstating One-Eye. She thought particularly highly of Faith Geer and George McGrath's performances, and David Beggs' Floyd Knowles, but felt some aspects of the production itself at variance with the script, that the acting tended too far in places towards naturalism whereas the writing veers towards the expressionistic.

My reaction to this is that although a longer script would probably draw more from the novel, I don't believe that not including the episodes she describes diminishes a two-hour studio version, where selection has to be extremely rigorous. The number of sequences included from the book is of less importance than what you do with them. And, of course, I would like to develop it further. But her comments on the production, being so close to Frank Gelati's, give food for thought. So many of the characters do bridge a naturalistic and non-naturalistic convention and the script is intended to be produced non-naturalistically, or weighted that way. Obviously, in her eyes and in Frank Gelati's, we have not entirely succeeded in striking that pitch. Or perhaps some of the acting has blurred since we opened . . .

Late tonight, on my way home, buy a copy of *Festival Times*, the weekly Festival newspaper published by Edinburgh University Publications. Of variable quality but lively and indispensable. Most of the contributors are students and it is a unique opportunity for people to begin writing and publishing. A complimentary if not particularly well-written review of the play in the 'First XI' section, telling the story and picking out Faith and George. Also an article about the company beneath that photograph taken in New York of Faith and Albert as Ma and Pa, staring into the camera, copies of which are in all the Press packs along with a couple of rehearsal shots.

Wednesday 19   No review of *The Grapes* on *Festival* *View* this morning.

Caption review, under the Faith and Albert picture, in *The Independent*. Generally unfavourable but contradicts itself with the last sentence.

Attacks the adaptation as 'a ponderous, reverential affair', but adds that it is hard to see how we could have done better and remained so faithful to the original. (Does this mean that the reviewer already thinks the *novel* is ponderous, etc?) Either the adaptation or the production (which, is not clear), is 'thin on tension as crisis succeeds crisis' and 'there is lots of very American naturalism in the performances.' (Is he making a similar point to those made by Frank Gelati and Adline Finlay?) But if so, that appears to be contradicted by the first part of the final sentence: 'Less a drama, more a showcase for the skills of American Festival Theatre' (which implies the adaptation is defective but the performances are not), and the entire piece is contradicted by the ending, the second and last part of the sentence: 'this Fringe First winner should be seen.'

Dispiriting.

To the *Kaleidoscope* office to record my *Troilus and Cressida* review. Wonder whether discreetly to put out feelers about the Monday chap to see what, if anything, comes back, but as soon as I arrive, I realise I needn't bother. For there he is. He's setting up the microphones and spooling the tapes onto the recording deck. He's the sound engineer. I say nothing. He says nothing.

Thursday 20   Still no *Festival View* review.

To the theatre at 9 a.m. A Grampian Television crew has arranged to record an extract from the play for a current affairs programme and require as many of the cast as possible to be present. I have agreed to represent Hal in some sort of hosting capacity, but feel that if the actors are good enough to work at this time in the morning, the least I can do is be there as moral support. When I arrive, the actors, in costume, are sitting in the auditorium, a lighting man is setting up lights on a tripod, a cameraman peering through a lens in the back row, a sound recordist sitting in the front, and a reporter shuffling about looking distracted. As the reporter has not seen the show, the choice of extract falls to the actors. Eventually we decide on part of the Act One homecoming scene and the cast take up positions on the stage. There is simultaneous movement from the lighting man, the cameraman, and reporter, but none whatever from the sound recordist. Small, solid, fair-haired, wearing a heavy blue anorak, he sits like a sack of potatoes in his seat, eyes closed, a cigarette clamped between his lips. He is very, inertly, drunk. At nine in the morning.

'I suppose you've, um . . . noticed the, er . . . sound chap?' murmurs the reporter.

'Yes. Yes, I have.'
'Bit embarrassing, really.'
It certainly is. The actors look dumbfounded.

It transpires that he is an alcoholic, a statement to which I can readily agree, though why he has been sent down from Aberdeen to a city in which, during the Festival at least, alcohol is available twenty-four hours a day to the dedicated, is beyond me.

The homecoming scene is set up. The television lights flashing on provoke a Pavlovian response from the sound man, who jerks upright, lugs the strap of the recorder over his shoulder, and – carrying a boom microphone like a spear – walks to the side of the auditorium, stopping when he collides with the wall. The cameraman moves forward, slips headphones over his skull, pushes buttons on the recorder, nips back to the camera, and shoots the scene in long shot. Then a close-up, the camera, lights, and recordist steered into position in front of the stage.

The reporter records a short interview with Albert while the actors are changing, before we troop outside to film, for some reason, the cast walking up the street and entering the foyer. Leaving the building is a hazardous exercise for the recordist, who takes the stairs up from the theatre hand on wall, three steps up and one down, struggling doggedly on like some over-loaded Sherpa determined to reach the summit with the rest of the expedition.

Do the outside shots, the sound man pointing the boom in what might vaguely be the right direction. I wonder what, if anything, will be shown on television.

Afterwards, over coffee and scones in the just-opened theatre restaurant, a talk on American theatre in Britain with Albert. (Americans – these Americans – love scones. They are rarely available in New York.) It is curious that at a time when British plays and musicals have found favour in New York, American plays are so well received in London. Odets, O'Neill, Mamet, Shepard, and Miller have all been produced in the West End and by the national companies during the past few years. He is especially interested in the British response to Arthur Miller. *The American Clock* was at the National Theatre while *The Archbishop's Ceiling* played at the RSC Barbican Pit at the end of 1986, and *A View from the Bridge* is currently selling out at the National. Miller, he says, has not such a high profile in New York, but Lanford Wilson (who is not widely known here) is produced and Sam Shepard is very popular.

Later, to a talk by playwright David Hare who, coincidentally, suggests an explanation for American success in London. Audiences today, he says, want to be emotionally as well as intellectually involved. They want to be moved. Audiences cheered *Pravda* (the enormously successful comedy about the state of the contemporary newspaper industry he co-authored with Howard Brenton) because it reflected their feelings about that situation. For him, there is a great need for plays, whatever they are saying, to be produced with a sense of aesthetic value and with performances that are emotionally absorbing. And in the audience at *A View from the Bridge* you can feel a high emotional charge from the stage.

A very favourable review in *The Listener*. Faith Geer is compared to O'Casey's Juno again and the company act with 'conviction, restraint and physical veracity'. For the production, 'jaunty snatches of music give way to torrents of rain and of weeping' and 'economy of design matches the adaptation, a model of compression and juxtaposition.'

Friday 21   *The Grapes* reviewed on *Festival View* this morning.

It appears to be a convention with this programme that the Festival is assumed to be predominantly serious and the Fringe predominantly fun, therefore Festival reviews, always on first, are each given three or four minutes while Fringe reviews are jostled together one to a minute and usually chuckled through. The Film Festival, a major international event, is always relegated to last place.

The musicals bloke comes on and gives a spirited run-down of a ragtime concert before being deflected onto *The Grapes*. Kicks off by announcing that it 'seems to be a play in its own right'. The word 'seems' must have pierced a built-up hyper-sensitivity as his following remark, 'I haven't read the book very recently, but it didn't *seem* to have any glaring omissions,' causes me to volubly lecture the radio, describing some of what is omitted in the play and generally sounding off against equivocation, so missing the rest of his piece.

Playing it back (I had recorded it), I discover that he had ended up quite chirpily: 'wonderful experience, brilliantly done, superb cast . . .' But I'm irked, first that a reviewer had not taken the trouble to do a bit of research and blithely admitted it to his listeners; second, that in describing the plot, he attributes a corporate motivation to the characters whereas I have taken great pains (as have Rob and the actors) to differentiate between them, and third, that there are parts of the play that do not appear in the book and I would be interested in someone's views about those.

I'm rapidly coming to the conclusion that the current state of theatre criticism is mediocre. It is not often that a critic writes – or broadcasts – from a knowledge of both literature and theatre. Most theatre criticism is actually literary criticism or entirely impressionistic, or the former with a bit of the latter thrown in. There are honourable exceptions, of course. And no critic can be conversant with the entire wealth and range of drama and dramatic forms, although editors and his readership expect him to be. And no critic would be human unless he or she enjoyed one writer, performance, style, whatever, more than another. But there is – must be – a level of being informed, receptive, and expressive below which it is unacceptable to fall. Reviewing plays myself, I have been guilty of all of this in the past, I know. But, as a writer with *The Grapes*, I am angry at feeling it has to be defended, not against opinion, but against reviewers whose approach is not what it should be and whose reviews are not authoritative.

Equilibrium restored by an interesting piece in *The Times Educational Supplement, Scotland*, in which the reviewer describes some of the aspirations embodied in the phrase the American Dream, and suggests the realities all too often become the American Nightmare, of which *The Grapes of Wrath* is one of the great works. It is complimentary to the play: 'the paring down which has been required strengthens the story in many ways and Steinbeck's sentimentality has largely been cut', and describes George McGrath's portrayal of Casy as 'entirely convincing in its complexity of thought and feeling', and Peter Spears' performance as 'strong'. I'm very pleased Peter's work has been given some recognition. The whole thing restores faith. A review with ideas.

To the BBC Radio Ulster lunch. Chris Spurr, his programme assistant, Owen Dudley Edwards, Michael Billington, Liz Lochhead (author of *Mary Queen of Scots Got Her Head Chopped Off*), Michael Barnes (director of the Belfast Festival), and myself. Liz and I apologise to each other for not having seen each other's play. Conversation, food, and wine.

To the theatre as the show comes down. Sue Ellen arrives to do some costume repair work. She says she had noticed a lack of men wearing pony-tails in London, and asks whether pony-tails are on the way in or the way out. Apparently, they are very much in in New York and she is in a quandary as to where the latest development has taken place. 'Hair,' she says, 'has a way of moving around. It gets hard to catch up with it.'

Tonight to the Berliner Ensemble's *The Caucasian Chalk Circle*. Absolutely within the Brecht tradition, the white half-curtain in front of the stage periodically drawn aside to reveal an open space surrounded by a light backcloth, earth-coloured, utilitarian props moved swiftly on and off, detached, serviceable (in the best sense of the word) playing and direction. I don't find it a strong play, but it is a very strong production.

The chap sitting next to us has travelled a long way especially to see this. 'I could kill for Brecht,' he says.

Saturday 22   An extensive and astonishingly generous review, with the Faith and Albert picture, in *The Financial Times*. A vigorous and meticulous account of the play, enthusiastically complimenting the adaptation and 'Rob Mulholland's masterly production'. Faith Geer is 'simple and truthful', Chris Ann Moore's 'an absolutely natural performance with a touch of the young Julie Harris', and the final image of Rose of Sharon nursing the starving man 'a picture that defies mawkishness and lingers in the memory like an icon, resonant, universal and triumphant'.

I am really quite shaken. A very good review can leave you feeling as vulnerable as a bad review. But I am very pleased for the company, especially for Rob and Chris Ann.

The BBC Radio Ulster programme goes smoothly, orchestrated by Chris Spurr with the precision of a military operation.

A very good day.

Sunday 23   A paragraph review in the *Mail on Sunday* – the play 'masterfully distils the essence of Steinbeck's angry novel . . .'

No reviews of the play in the heavies, *The Sunday Times* or *The Observer*. Frustratingly, both tend to stick to the Traverse and the Assembly Rooms. Particularly *The Observer*, whose reviewer is the leading Traverse fan.

With Vivien to Stormfield Theatre's *Hauptmann*. An intensely compulsive piece beginning with a monologue by Hauptmann himself sitting in his prison cell. The play opens out into broader narration by other characters interspersed by very short naturalistically acted scenes: Lindbergh comforting his distraught wife, a man lighting his way by torch as he makes his way to a night-time rendezvous with the man who might be the kidnapper. The second act is almost conventional court-room drama, Hauptmann being examined and cross-examined on the stand. What the play does is to take well-used, even perhaps outmoded conventions, but fashion them for its own ends. It is an exceptional piece of writing by John Logan, and a terrific company performance led by Denis P. O'Hare in the title role, small, wiry, tense, Germanic.

Tonight, to the Pittsburgh Symphony Orchestra, conducted by Lorin Maazel. Schubert, Gershwin's piano concerto in F played by Patricia Prattis Jennings, and *An American in Paris*. Sit in the organ gallery behind the orchestra, and so watch an extraordinarily expressive conductor full-face.

Monday 24   Birmingham Rep and a London fringe theatre have both expressed an interest in the play, and representatives of a Swedish theatre came to the performance today. There are, of course, a lot of scouts in town during the Festival, going to see a lot of shows, and each year some of the best Fringe plays are invited to the Donmar Warehouse in London in the autumn. That would, of course, be impossible for us: we only have permission to stage the play for a limited run in Edinburgh.

The Depression photographs, by the way, have arrived, and are hanging in the foyer. Black-and-white images of children staring from the backs of trucks, bewildered men and women . . .

Tuesday 25   Brief, mildly favourable mention of *The Grapes* in the *Glasgow Herald*. Not that many people at the Edinburgh Festival read the *Glasgow Herald* . . .

Go to the play today, to have another look at the production and to see if and how the performances have changed.

The first part of Act One, after the tableau and Tom's opening speech, is now very light, too light, Tom and Casy's Scene Two meeting particularly so. Alarmingly so. Moreover, the humour in this and the following homecoming scene is being searched out, pointed up and gestured through, rather than just being *there*, and a kind of jauntiness permeates each sequence like a spreading polluting stain as the play proceeds. It continues, in fact, as far as Scene Six, when the Joads meet the Wilsons after they stop for the night just outside Bethany. Their meeting has become almost as jovial as one between relations rather than what it used to be, the initially circumspect amicability of strangers thrown together by chance. Perhaps one reason for this is that the cast are now *too* at ease with the play. Another may be that they know audiences relish the later Ma and Pa confrontations and are looking to play the earlier, more discreet interchanges too expansively. Although Faith Geer's performance has authoritative weight, there is an overall loss of subtlety and dramatic balance and the play only pulls itself into a different register before the Granma death sequence, and the process of it doing so is, to me, very apparent. The remainder of the Act holds firm, the jack-handle scene confident and controlled, the leaving of the Wilsons poignant and unhurried.

Act Two has strengthened considerably. Persky and Bird, outwardly reasonable, have a core of real prejudice and menace, and the Hooverville sequence is taut with anger. The Act is still flawed, in my eyes, by the writing and the inclusion of the Rose of Sharon–Young Girl scene and, although no reviewers have commented on this one way or another, I wish I could go back to it and re-work it. In fact, no reviewers so far have remarked at all on the efficacy or otherwise of Persky and Bird, or Rose of Sharon betraying Tom, which I find rather surprising, or have suggested that anything in the play needs re-working, although there are several pieces, given the chance, I would want to have a look at. One is the place of Tom Joad in the central section, from Act One, Scene Eight, after the jack-handle sequence, through to the first portion of Act Two, where Tom could possibly be built up a little more significantly. Not that I believe he fades at the moment, but I think it is Peter Spears' stage presence as much as anything that keeps Tom so apparent here. Perhaps there could be a more decisive through-line, that's all. Just a thought.

Another is that Mrs Thomas, the ranch owner who appears briefly in Act Two, would revert to Mr Thomas, as originally written. Although Sandy Spatz has put in a great deal of work into the part, and Rob and Albert assured us there were female ranch owners in California, to me it remains a casting compromise, although, again, no reviewer has called attention to it.

Pleased to see that the humour of Pa's indignation as Ma assumes the position of family organiser at Weedpatch and Hooper's Ranch is not played up at all, although the audience clearly enjoys it. The play does need a judiciously placed humour, or rather, a rough buoyancy, a consequence of the characters discovering their strengths and weaknesses in their reactions to the situation in which they find themselves, but not a levity that has no discernible anchor in the tenor of the piece. The heifer story, for example, even though it serves a purpose in the play, is slightly disconnected from it, which is maybe why it does not get the audience response the Ma and Pa interchanges do.

The final section, from the boxcar scenes to the ending in the barn, has gained in stature since the play opened, and each performance carries a finely judged and sustained emotional impact in this small theatre. The world, at one point, seems to revolve around Ma Joad, shifts to Rose of Sharon, and finally to Tom himself. Chris Ann has made great inroads into her role, but the cumulative effect is of an ensemble piece. What we always wanted. Again, a silence after the lights fade down and the storm sound snaps off in the darkness, and then a very warm audience response. The actors take three bows this time.

But I'm worried about that first fifteen minutes or so. It is beginning to drift and should be caught. I talk to Duncan about it. He promises to go to the performance tomorrow to see for himself and, if he agrees with me, we'll have a word with Jodi.

Wednesday 26 Duncan agrees. Jodi gives appropriate notes to the cast.

Complimentary though weakly-written review in the *Evening News*, and a feature interview with Hal in the *Glasgow Herald*. Quote: 'We come over for two months, rehearse in London, do workshops with the Royal Shakespeare Company, and then put the shows together and hang our hides on a pole.'

A less florid interview with Albert (Albert Bennett metamorphosing through a printing error, *presumably* through a printing error, into Arnold Bennett) in *Festival Times*, in which Arnold, or Albert, says that the budget for the American Festival Theatre Edinburgh season this year was 100,000 dollars.

Quite a proportion of that went on *The Grapes* . . .

Saw *The Observer* critic (not the main one, his deputy) walking purposefully into the Assembly Rooms this afternoon. Of course. I spoke to the reviewer for *Plays Magazine* the other day. She was on her way to the Traverse . . .

Tonight to the *Kunju Macbeth*, performed by the Shanghai Kunju Theatre. An extraordinary experience. The English surtitles projected above the stage appear to be a literal translation of a very bad Chinese translation of the play, so that while the plot and even a few of the words are intermittently recognisable, Shakespeare's text is largely not.

It is performed almost at a run and half-shouted, half-sung in warbling headtone to a strident percussion orchestra. Clashing cymbals and cracking woodblocks. The production, therefore, is played to an incessant chung-chung-bang-bang-chung-ch-ch-chung! It is immensely colourful and some of it spectacular: two jabbering white-haired witches somersault from the sleeves of a third and monkey-figures caper through scenes of banner-bedecked pageantry; some of it, such as the sleepwalking scene, is lyrically beautiful.

Thursday 27   A very good review in *The Stage*, again with the Faith and Albert picture. Adaptation 'very skilful', Faith Geer's Ma 'strongly-drawn', 'idealism is powerfully voiced in George McGrath's portrayal of Casy' and 'Rob Mulholland's tight direction never falters'. The production is 'of strong authenticity and sustained force' and the performance 'highly accomplished, always forceful and altogether a memorable success'.

Also hear a tape of the *Meridian* programme that was broadcast on World Service last Friday, the presenter describing the play as 'one of the hits of this year's Fringe'.

Check on the performance this afternoon. Relieved to find the first portion back on course again, played with conviction and control.

Brilliant sunshine today, but the streets, though still crowded, are perceptibly less busy. Several Fringe shows played only the first two weeks of the Festival and closed last Saturday. This is partly because many companies cannot afford to come for the full three weeks (and this year, as every year, some left within days because their shows failed), and also that when the Festival used to run during the last two weeks of August and the first week of September, the third week was always thought of as being very quiet. The Festival has only recently been brought forward to run during the last three weeks of August, and the third week has consequently picked up. In fact, one company are coming from Ireland to give one performance only of *The Playboy of the Western World*, this Saturday, the last day of the Fringe. So, the free daily diary still lists hundreds of Fringe shows from early morning to late night and beyond and Festival concerts and plays are sold out, but with the Film and Book Festivals having ended, things are beginning to wind down a little. *The Grapes*, though, is safely booked out and has been since

Monday, and there are returns queues every day, so the third week is proving to be good for us.

With Vivien tonight to see *The Nutcracker*, performed by the National Ballet of Finland, choreographed by Yuri Grigorovich. Something of a Dickensian Christmas look, and the idea of a fairy tale as a metaphor of adult life is explored with a direct and simple clarity.

As the lights go down for the second act, notice a tall, elderly man and a middle-aged woman taking their places in a box near the stage. He sits, smoothing his tie, then rubbing the palms of his hands back along his balding head. She sits hunched beside him, flaxen hair falling past her shoulders, staring intently at the stage. Sir Rudolf Bing and his wife.

Manager of Glyndebourne before and after the war, he founded the Edinburgh Festival in 1947 and was its director until 1949, when he left to become General Manager of the New York Metropolitan Opera House, from 1950–72. After the war, a campaign was launched to found a new arts festival in Europe and, so the story goes, emerging one evening from the Caledonian Hotel, Bing was so impressed by the sight of the castle on its crag overlooking the city, that he resolved the festival should be held in Edinburgh.

He is now 85, the Festival, and the Fringe, 41. Eight companies arrived unannounced in Edinburgh for that first spontaneous Fringe; this year there were over eight hundred listed in the programme guide.

Recently, there have been newspaper reports of Sir Rudolf's frailty and the couple's almost nomadic life, their checking in and out of hotels and guesthouses, their depending on the help of friends and benefactors. Edinburgh owes him so much. Apparently, he very, very rarely visits the Festival he helped create.

By the time the dancers appear for their curtain call, the couple in the box have gone.

Friday 28   I feel as though I am almost at the end of a long journey.

Saturday 29   The last peformance of *The Grapes of Wrath*.

Afterwards, in the theatre, the cast open the huge bottle of champagne Duncan and I bought them after the first performance three weeks ago. The feeling of achievement that the play, now known to the actors as *The Angry Raisins*, did so well, and the regret that it is now all over and everyone involved will be going their separate ways, is tempered by a sudden tiredness. The actors have been working away from home for two months, and being at the Festival makes you doubly tired when you stop. They stand on the stage taking photographs, or sit, elbows on knees, in the front row seats, talking about what happens next.

Damien Kavanagh is going to tour Scotland for a day or two and see some countryside. Others are going straight back to the United States. Faith Geer will be auditioning in New York. Paul Binotto is considering joining a national tour of *Les Misérables*, and looking forward to continuing work on his Ovid project. George McGrath, who, with his straying grey hair, baggy shirts and neckscarves, has begun to look like Jim Casy off stage as well as on, has bought a large, battered leather suitcase from a junk-shop for 25p, and he and Miranda are proudly showing it off. They leave for New York at 8.30 tomorrow morning and once there, Miranda will return to school and George will prepare for his one-man play. Chris Ann Moore is heading back to Chicago and 'audition, audition, call back, audition, audition, call back, cast, act, audition, audition . . .' Peter Spears is starting his homeward journey tonight: sitting up on the Nightrider train from Edinburgh to London, transferring to Heathrow (where he plans to sleep), to get a plane for Chicago later in the day, then another from Chicago to Kansas City. Twenty-four hours of travelling. Albert Bennett is going back to New York having achieved full nights of sleep in Edinburgh. We talk over what we know of Steppenwolf's plans for their version of *The Grapes of Wrath*. Already, Albert is speculating on what American Festival Theatre might bring to the Festival next year.

We drink toasts, champagne from plastic cups. To each other. To John Steinbeck.

To John Steinbeck.

Sunday 30   The last reviews. Nothing in *The Sunday Times* or *The Observer*, but an interesting note in the *Sunday Telegraph*, whose reviewer thought the play 'the best Fringe offering of my third week', and the performances 'ensemble playing of remarkable selflessness'. He puts forward the idea, however, that although the adaptation 'cannot conceal the sentimental falsity of Steinbeck's assumption that the fact of being poor, humble and exploited somehow, of itself, endows people with virtue, it succeeds in bringing out all the generosity of spirit of a sometimes muddled writer'. Interesting, because I hoped we had rescued the play from the sentimentality of the novel. *The Financial Times*, in fact, thought the production 'eschews sentimentality', and several reviews commented on its harshness ... Wonder idly whether sentimentality is inextricably bound up with 'generosity of spirit', but feel too tired ...

We were mentioned on *Critics Forum*, the BBC Radio 3 arts review programme, last night. *The Observer* film critic described the play as 'immensely moving'; it 'bears comparison with, and is in fact tougher than, John Ford's classic film'.

SEPTEMBER

Tuesday 1   The Festival and Fringe is over. At
the Royal Scots Club, lighting scaffolding is dismantled. The streets are
comparatively deserted. Already, it seems, the year is turning. I am
looking forward to getting away for a few days.

Hal, Graham, and I take the stage set out of the Netherbow Theatre.
Label everything with a note of to where it has to be delivered. Load
everything into a rented van. Leave behind a bare stage, an empty
theatre.